MIDDLE SCHOOL ART:
ISSUES OF CURRICULUM AND INSTRUCTION

Carole Henry, Editor
University of Georgia

1996

The National Art Education Association

About NAEA

Founded in 1947, the National Art Education Association is the largest professional art education association in the world. Membership includes elementary and secondary teachers, art administrators, museum educators, arts council staff, and university professors from throughout the United States and 66 foreign countries. NAEA's mission is to advance art education through professional development, service, advancement of knowledge and leadership.

Cover: Arthur Garfield Dove. *Untitled* (formally known as *League of Nations*), circa 1910. Pastel on thin paper mounted on pulp board. 21-5/16" x 17-13/16". Georgia Museum of Art, The University of Georgia, Eva Underhill Holbrook Memorial Collection of American Art, Gift of Alfred H. Holbrook. Photograph by Michael McKelvey.

ISBN 0-937652-78-4

TABLE OF CONTENTS

Introduction

Art education is emerging from a period of introspection and redefinition that has significantly affected how art is taught in the schools. The efforts of those committed to broadening the base of art education through discipline-based and multicultural instructional approaches are now visible throughout the field. An increasing number of art teachers at all grade levels are working on a daily basis to design instruction providing students with opportunities to create and respond to works of art. The importance of art education as an area of inquiry through which critical thinking skills can be developed and practiced is also influencing curriculum development. This volume will examine these and other contemporary issues of curriculum and instruction intrinsic to art education specifically at the middle school level.

Although middle schools vary in grade level composition, generally educators include grades five through eight in this category. The middle school child undergoes significant physical and mental changes during adolescence, and a sensitivity on the part of the teacher to the accompanying emotions and intellectual needs is essential for successful instruction. The art room can become a safe, nurturing environment where students from various economic and cultural backgrounds learn to think creatively, develop confidence in themselves, and explore ideas that are important to all of us. In order to provide this kind of environment, art educators must understand the varying needs, interests, and capabilities of the middle school student. Program content and instructional strategies for effective teaching should reflect such understanding.

The authors represented in this anthology have each addressed specific issues of teaching art at the middle school level which can enlighten and guide middle school curriculum development and instructional approaches. While some articles are theoretical in nature, others are based on application and observation in middle

Carole Henry
University of Georgia

school art classrooms. Emphasis throughout the volume has been placed on the communication of instructional content and the recognition of the needs and interests of the students.

Eugene Harrison provides an introductory overview of the developmental needs and characteristics of adolescents and discusses the components of a discipline-based instructional approach as being especially suited to this age group. He seeks to establish a curricular framework that successfully bridges the gap between elementary and high school art instruction. Additionally, Harrison summarizes recently published textbooks in the field that he has found to be helpful in curriculum development.

Anne Wolcott and **Renee Miller** report on a curricular unit which they developed to meet the specific developmental needs of middle school students. The unit was developed around the theme of "the self," a topic of extreme importance to adolescents, and included instruction reflective of a discipline-based approach. Wolcott and Miller have continued to refine the unit as it has been implemented over time with middle school students. They believe that the success of this instructional approach confirms that the intellectual content of art can be integrated into the middle school curriculum, and they stress the importance of connections for students to other areas of knowledge.

Alice Arnold advocates using the art of storytelling as motivation with younger adolescents. As she explains, stories give young people "access to their emotional lives by illustrating problem-solving situations that mirror many of the dilemmas that they may encounter." Arnold relates the use of literature to inspire a group mural and discusses how works of art were used to explore historical and aesthetic issues throughout the project.

Andra Nyman presents a rationale for the inclusion of a multicultural approach to art education as a means for helping adolescents better understand themselves and the world around them. Nyman emphasizes teaching for understanding through the integration of the content of art appreciation, art history, and artistic heritage. The chapter provides a persuasive argument that a multicultural approach to teaching art can better prepare students for the economic, political, social, and ethical issues that will confront them throughout their lives.

Mary Stokrocki describes how one particular middle school teacher successfully integrated multicultural art history instruction into daily studio teaching of seventh grade art students. The chapter provides insights into the use of humor and concern as important aspects of effective motivation of middle school students and illustrates the importance of establishing connections between important concepts and the lives of the students. Stockrocki emphasizes teaching for cultural understanding and concludes with specific recommendations that can help foster increased student involvement.

Mary Erickson explores the ability of sixth-graders to develop art historical understanding in terms of the students' levels of aesthetic development. The students received art history instruction organized around cross-cultural themes supported with related art production activities throughout the school year. Erickson interviewed selected students periodically and, using Michael Parson's work as a guide, analyzed student understanding. She found that inquiry-oriented instruction was successful in helping the sixth graders develop a range of inquiry strategies resulting in greater aesthetic understanding than would normally be expected.

Gaye Leigh Green presents a semiotic approach to art criticism directed toward discussion of the work of art in terms of the artist, the image, and the perceiver. Green uses a painting by Lenora Carrington to illustrate how this approach can work in the art classroom. She believes that this approach is especially well-suited to the developing intellectual abilities of middle school students and can be easily adapted to meet individual curricular needs.

Marilyn Wolf-Ragatz reports on an extended museum experience involving sixth grade art students that can serve as a model for museum and school collaboration. In this particular program, the students were able to meet the exhibiting artist and to work closely with a professional poet as they developed their own interpretive poems in response to individual works of art. The project culminated in a museum reception and the publication of a book of poetry and illustrations by the students. The description of the planning process and the program structure will be especially helpful to other art teachers interested in using art museums as educational resources.

Rosalind Ragans and **Bunyan Morris** provide valuable insights into motivational approaches and classroom management strategies gained from their extensive experiences working with middle school students. Their ideas are grounded in an intuitive understanding and appreciation of the nature and special needs of adolescents and can help minimize the frustrations middle school art teachers commonly experience.

Carol Stavropoulos advocates the use of grid drawing techniques to help middle school students develop confidence in their own drawing abilities and in themselves as individuals. She documents her successful use of this technique with a problematic student and provides numerous suggestions for creative grid drawing assignments which go beyond skill acquisition and also incorporate art historical content.

George Szekely calls our attention to the often neglected need of the middle school student to participate in socially acceptable forms of play. He believes that such forms of play can readily become part of the art curriculum and that this rediscovered joy can motivate adolescents toward creative thought and artistic production. Szekely's thinking reflects a keen understanding of the middle school child and can help all of us become more sensitive to our students.

Susan Witten addresses the topic of art education for students with special needs within the context of the middle school art classroom. She provides an overview of the history of legislation leading to the practices of mainstreaming and inclusion and gives practical and informed suggestions as to how to better create an equal opportunity classroom.

Eldon Katter discusses the topic of assessment in the art classroom as outlined at numerous teacher inservice workshops that he and **Marilyn Stewart** have conducted. Eight central questions are presented and are designed to serve as guidelines for teachers beginning to develop their own assessment plans. The basic premise is that valid assessment strategies will result in improvements in both teaching and learning. Katter's and Stewart's approach is consistent for all grade levels.

Appreciation is extended to all of the contributing authors for their interest in and support of this volume. The writers have articulated, in very individual ways, their deep commitment to the importance of art education in the middle school years. I also value the personal knowledge I gained as a middle school art teacher and am indebted to all of my former students who "educated" me. Credit must also be given to W. Robert Nix who taught me long ago that the most important thing about teaching is the students we teach and to Edmund Burke Feldman who introduced me to the value of teaching from works of art long before it became prevalent in the field. I especially want to thank Andra Nyman for her continued encouragement, Lori Resler for her editorial assistance, and Felicia Bush for her long hours of reference checks, editorial insights, and dedicated keyboard assistance. Most importantly, I also want to express my gratitude to the National Art Education Association for making this project possible.

The Nature of the Middle School Learner: Implications for Art Instruction

Eugene R. Harrison
Eastern Illinois University

For many students, entering middle school marks the first opportunity for art instruction taught by an art specialist. It is regretful that discrepancies sometimes occur between an understanding of the characteristics of early adolescent students, middle school curricula, and recognized pedagogical applications (Biehler & Snowman, 1990; Eccles & Midgley, 1989; Hillman, Wood, Becker, & Altier, 1990; Jackson & Hornbeck, 1989). As a result, some middle school art teachers approach art instruction either as an extension of the elementary art program or as an introductory high school art course, with little regard to the special needs of middle school students.

This chapter will present appropriate art instructional content and methodology for the middle school level. A well-planned middle school art curriculum should provide students with challenging in-depth approaches to making and understanding art. A discipline-based approach in teaching art can bridge the gap between the mental processes, peer interactions, and art activities typical in the elementary grades to those more sophisticated ones found in high school. A discipline-based approach also offers middle school students opportunities for intellectual, personal, and artistic growth.

The unique characteristics and needs of the middle school child necessitate that a middle school art program should guide students toward the following:

1. Becoming aware of the processes and problems that artists, art historians, art critics, and aestheticians encounter.
2. Developing self-confidence in their abilities to create artwork.
3. Becoming comfortable relating to their peers through group and individual art activities.
4. Acquiring knowledge about the content of art production, art history, art criticism, and aesthetics.

5. Beginning to assume more academic responsibility and to endeavor to become creative problem-solvers (National Art Education Association, 1972; Michael, 1983).

CHARACTERISTICS OF EARLY ADOLESCENCE

Adolescence can be divided into three stages: early adolescence (ages 10 through 14), middle adolescence (ages 15 through 17), and late adolescence (ages 18 to adulthood). A key characteristic of this developmental period is the lack of clear boundaries between the beginning and end of adolescence making it difficult for young people to determine when they cease being children and become young adults.

Since middle school age students, grades 5 through 8 (ages 10 through 14), typify early adolescence, their needs as addressed through art activities are the focus of this chapter. Uniquely, middle school students are characterized by a broad range of variability that is far greater than the individual differences typically found in either elementary or high school students (Toepher, 1990).

An obvious and significant variable involves physical developmental differences. Because girls usually have a growth spurt at age 11 and experience puberty shortly thereafter, they typically have a height and weight advantage upon entering early adolescence. Boys, because of their later physical maturation (typically having a growth spurt at age 13 and experiencing puberty by age 14), quickly achieve and begin to surpass the early height and weight advantage of girls (Hillman, 1991).

During early adolescence, intellectual development progresses rapidly, resulting in an increase in the knowledge base in terms of specific content as well as an increase in mental-processing capabilities. Students experience increases in long- and short-term memory and attention span; in addition, specific processing strategies emerge during this time. Early adolescence marks a qualitative change from concrete to more formal and abstract ways of reasoning, with concrete thinking skills being gradually replaced by more abstract strategies involving hypothesis testing, the formation of naive "ideals," and multiple ways of problem-solving (Hillman, 1991).

Another variable impacting early adolescence is social-emotional development. The ongoing development of a sense of self-identity is a major characteristic of adolescence. This struggle for a sense of self is characterized by active exploration of social and personal interactions culminating in a personal value system and a sense of self which guides behavior. Common concerns include the uncertainty of the future, academics and school activities, peer pressure, appearance, and feelings of inferiority and loneliness (Hillman, 1991).

To help middle school students adjust to their physical, intellectual, and social-emotional changes, art educators must be cognizant of the specific needs of this age group and devise appropriate and relevant

Adolescence can be divided into three stages: early adolescence (ages 10 through 14), middle adolescence (ages 15 through 17), and late adolescence (ages 18 to adulthood).

art instruction. A discipline-based approach to the teaching of art can help middle school students adjust to adolescence by challenging their intellectual and artistic development, helping them develop confidence in themselves and their artwork, and guiding them as they interact with peers.

DISCIPLINE-BASED ART EDUCATION AND THE MIDDLE SCHOOL ART CURRICULUM

As envisioned, discipline-based art education is an approach to art instruction that incorporates learning from the four art domains (art production, art history, art criticism, and aesthetics) to give students an increasingly sophisticated understanding and appreciation of art. The study of art is considered a discipline within general education with content presented sequentially and cumulatively within the curriculum. Instructional content and modes of inquiry from the four art domains are taught interactively to build a multifaceted approach that engages students' abilities to respond to, understand, create, and appreciate art objects (Clark, Day, & Greer, 1987; Dobbs, 1992; Greer, 1984).

The Role of Art Production
The studio activity should be an integral part of a discipline-based approach. This instructional model is presented with the studio activity as the culminating activity in which the introductory discussion uses concepts from art history, art criticism, and aesthetics to motivate in-depth understanding and enriched art studio participation.

Art studio instruction should assist middle school students in creating artwork in order to understand the processes artists experience when making art, to gain technical skills and knowledge in working with media and techniques, and to develop self-confidence in expressing feelings and emotions through media and techniques.

The Role of Art History
With discipline-based art instruction, middle school students can learn to apply art historical modes of inquiry as they discover information about works of art (Clark et al., 1987). Using art historical modes of inquiry as a model, students can come to understand a work of art in terms of when, where, and by whom the work was created. They can identify the unique features (artistic style) of a work compared to features found in other works, discover how artists are influenced by the world around them, and make a decision about a work's importance in the history of art (Mittler,1989).

Well-planned art history instruction should provide middle school students with the opportunity to learn what processes art historians use to study works of art, how works of art reflect the beliefs and values of various cultures throughout time, why artists create works of art, and why we value works of art.

...art educators must be cognizant of the specific needs of this age group and devise appropriate and relevant art instruction.

The Role of Art Criticism

Art critics clarify the meaning of works of art and evaluate their quality. Feldman (1970) outlined a process to help students examine and better understand an artwork before making an evaluation of its quality. Feldman's model incorporates four steps in the examination of an artwork: description, analysis, interpretation, and judgment. Students are guided sequentially through the four stages, examining facts and ideas before making judgmental decisions about the artwork.

During the first stage, description, students describe the work of art through identification of subject matter and art elements. Teachers ask questions such as, "What objects do you see in the work?", "Can you describe them for us?", or "What different kinds of lines do you see?"

Analysis is a continuation of description but focuses on the way the artist has organized the elements of art within the work. In this stage, students are asked to look at and describe the various ways that design elements and principles have been used by the artist. Questions can be asked such as, "What area or shape do you notice first?", "How has the artist used repetition to create unity?", "What makes the work appear to be balanced?", or "How does the way the artist used value give you a sense of space?"

Interpretation is an effort to find meaning in the artwork. Students should be guided by the information gleaned from description and analysis to formulate an interpretation that can be defended by the visual evidence. Teachers should help the students find relationships to their own lives as they engage in this process. Students can be reminded of similar experiences in their lives and then be guided to discuss the content of the work of art. Questions such as, "If you could be anywhere in this landscape, where would you choose to be and why?", "Would you want to meet this person?", or "Would you like to have this person for a teacher?" can help encourage middle school students to venture interpretations.

Judgment involves deciding on the value and significance of the artwork. Students can be asked to explain how a particular artwork compares to others of the same type. For example, students could be asked questions such as, "How does the way this landscape is painted compare to the landscape we saw at the museum?" or "Which of these self-portraits is most successful in terms of showing us how the artist felt?" The reasons given should be appropriate for the particular work of art (Mittler, 1989; Salome, 1984). Student reasons for deciding on the value of an artwork can also include criteria based on one or more of three basic philosophical theories of art: Imitationalism, Formalism, or Emotionalism. Although other theories can also be explored, these three provide a good foundation for supporting aesthetic judgments and can be easily grasped by the middle school student.

When students say that an artwork is successful because it looks like something in the real world, they are concentrating on evaluating the literal qualities of a work (those qualities that represent subject matter realistically). These students are using criteria intrinsic to the Imitationalism theory as they engage in judgment.

Students can be encouraged to concentrate on the visual qualities of a work (those qualities that represent the elements and principles of art) and assume a Formalist perspective. Students might say that an artwork is successful because the artist has used the elements and principles of art to create a unified and interesting work of art.

Students may also make judgments based on the expressive qualities in an artwork (those qualities that effectively communicate a feeling or mood to the viewer). For example, students will often say that a work is successful because it communicates a specific feeling (Mittler & Howze, 1989).

Students can learn to apply the four components of the critical process to their own and their classmates' work as well as to works of art. Whereas class discussions can introduce students to art criticism, written responses can provide individual practice and serve to document student progress. Some teachers have developed art criticism games that entertain as well as instruct.

Art criticism instruction should aid middle school students in learning about the processes art critics use to make evaluations about works of art and how to apply these processes to formulate interpretations of works of art. Students can also learn to transfer these critical processes to evaluate their own artworks or that of their peers and be introduced to the aesthetic criteria typically used to evaluate the quality of works of art.

The Role of Aesthetics

A frequently debated topic in current art education literature is the concept of aesthetics, with debate centering on such fundamental issues relevant to the art educator as, "What is aesthetics?" and "How should it be taught?" Simply stated, *aesthetics* is the branch of philosophy that questions the very nature of art. Aesthetic ideas are so influential in the art world and society that they permeate artistic notions and influence content relative to art history, art criticism, and art production. For example, aestheticians ask questions such as, "What is the true function of art?", "Does criteria exist for distinguishing good art from bad art?", "Can a natural object be a work of art?", or "What is the difference between fine art and crafts?" Answers to these questions have influenced the ever-evolving perceptions of art (Lankford, 1986; Crawford, 1987).

How can complex concepts about aesthetics be taught to middle school students? One avenue frequently used is to ask questions and discuss with students philosophical questions that relate to the visual arts. Crawford (1987) identifies five clusters of concepts normally attributed to aesthetics: (1) the art object, (2) appreciation and interpretation, (3) critical evaluation, (4) artistic creation, and (5) culture concept. Art educators can address these five concepts through questions designed to encourage thoughtful response and stimulated discussion.

Simply stated, aesthetics is the branch of philosophy that questions the very nature of art.

Teaching the concept of *the art object* can encompass discussions focused on the differences between works of art and other things. Questions such as, "What is a work of art?", "How can a work of art be distinguished from other objects?", or "In printmaking we consider the prints works of art, but why don't we consider the original plates works of art?" can help students formulate their own definitions of art.

Teaching the concept of *appreciation and interpretation* can involve the discussion of various meanings and interpretations of the artwork. Questions such as, "Why do you appreciate this work of art and not this one?" or "What makes your interpretation of a work of art better than another?" can assist students in reflecting about their beliefs about works of art.

Teaching the concept of *critical evaluation* can entail ideas that go beyond art criticism and include discussion about whether critical judgments of works of art can be supported by valid reasons. Students can be asked to think about the criteria they use in determining if a work of art is good; for example, "Explain why you think this work is good" or "Can you give reasons why you think this image is not a work of art?" Thoughtful deliberation activities teach students to justify their qualitative reasons about attributes of works of art.

Teaching the concept of *artistic creation* can include discussions involving reflective thinking about the process of making art. Questions can be asked such as, "Why do you enjoy making artwork?", "Why do you think people make art?", or "What qualities do you think make a person an artist?"

Teaching the concept of *cultural context* can involve discussing the idea that art does not exist in a vacuum and that the origins and valuing of works of art are integrated within society and culture. Questions such as, "Should art ever be censored? Why?", "Does art have to be beautiful, or can it be disturbing?", or "What purpose should art serve for society?" cause students to ponder art's relationship to society and culture (Battin, Fisher, Moore, & Silvers, 1989).

Instruction in aesthetics should assist middle school students in learning how and why aestheticians (past and present) examine the nature of art, how the purposes of art have changed throughout time, and how art, within the cultural context, has been influenced by society.

How Does It All Work Together? Putting Theory into Practice

One strategy for successfully implementing discipline-based art instruction is through the use of the discussion mode of presentation. During the introduction of a lesson, the art teacher can use the presentation and discussion of related art history, art criticism, and aesthetic concepts to challenge students to use higher-order art thinking skills (Bloom, Engelhart, Furst, Hill, & Krathwohl, 1956; Hamblen, 1984) and to motivate students to become actively engaged in the art production stage of the activity. Initially, questions can be used to introduce students to exemplary works of art and to help students refine their perceptual skills. Follow-up questions can help students

Thoughtful deliberation activities teach students to justify their qualitative reasons about attributes of works of art.

attend to details and make comparisons as they develop art vocabulary and art-thinking skills. The responses to each question naturally lead to different questions, and gradually the questions can become more focused, helping the students better understand key concepts.

After the introductory discussion, technical and procedural information necessary for art production can be presented. Even after the students are engaged in the studio activity, the art teacher should continue to reinforce prior concepts and introduce additional relevant issues for discussion to expand the students' knowledge of art history, art criticism, and aesthetics as well as art production.

Throughout the lesson, continual review and reinforcement of key concepts can serve to emphasize the conceptual consistency that is the hallmark of a discipline-based curriculum (Rush, 1987). Finally, during the concluding stages of the lesson, the art teacher should bring the lesson to meaningful closure summarizing what the students have learned and preparing them for the next lesson.

Textbook Resources for the Middle School Level
Since the mid-eighties, a number of excellent middle school art textbooks have been published. Each textbook approaches the teaching of art to middle school students differently: *Art in Action* (Hubbard, 1986) presents a studio emphasis; *Understanding and Creating Art* (Goldstein, Katz, Kowalchuk, & Saunders, 1986) involves an in-depth art historical investigation of selective artwork; *Exploring Art* (Mittler & Ragans, 1992a) has a comprehensive studio emphasis; *Understanding Art* (Mittler & Ragans, 1992b) uses the study of art history as the focus, and *A World of Images* (Chapman, 1992b) and *Art: Images and Ideas* (Chapman, 1992a) present a balanced studio and art-history approach. The texts are each identified as encompassing a discipline-based approach and contribute ideas and instructional suggestions which can serve as references for the art educator as well as textbooks for middle school students.

Art in Action (Hubbard, 1986) is a discipline-based art education textbook series written for use in the seventh and eighth grades. The texts are marketed as a continuation of the *Art in Action* series for grades one through six. The main goal of the program is to instruct students in understanding art, creating art, and appreciating art.

Each book consists of approximately 95 lessons with each lesson formatted into four key sections: (a) "Observing and Thinking Creatively" presents art vocabulary, art historical/critical information, and studio information; (b) "Instructions for Creating Art" provides step-by-step guidelines for creating an art work (c) "Art Materials and Equipment" identifies and describes the necessary art materials; and (d) a "Strand Diagram" suggests alternative subsequent assignments.

Understanding and Creating Art (Goldstein et al., 1986) is a two-volume discipline-based art education textbook series. The content and activities of each text are focused on specific works of art: the first addresses Grant Wood's *American Gothic* and Winslow Homer's *Gulf Stream,* and the other textbook includes Edward Hicks' *The*

...the art teacher should bring the lesson to meaningful closure summarizing what the students have learned and preparing them for the next lesson.

The intent of this chapter has been to provide suggestions for the implementation of a discipline—based approach in the teaching of art to middle school students.

Peaceable Kingdom, Emanuel Leutze's *Washington Crossing the Delaware*, and Joseph Stella's *The Brooklyn Bridge*.

Exploring Art (Mittler & Ragans, 1992a) utilizes an integrated approach to art production, art history, art criticism, and aesthetics. The text emphasizes the use of art media, but students are introduced to aesthetic theory, the elements and principles of art, art criticism, and art history before they explore various art media. There are two types of lessons, narrative and studio, within the text. The narrative lessons present art concepts and include a brief studio activity. The studio lessons present in-depth studio activities, build on prior studio experiences, and concentrate on the use of various art media and techniques.

Understanding Art (Mittler & Ragans, 1992b) is a companion text to *Exploring Art* and emphasizes a study of the history of art. Students are introduced to different aesthetic theories, the elements and principles of art, and art criticism before making an in-depth study of art history. Each lesson is supported by an appropriate and reinforcing studio activity.

A continuation of Laura Chapman's Discover Art Program, 1-6, includes two texts for grades seven and eight, *A World of Images* (1992b) and *Art: Images and Ideas* (1992a). Presented as part of a balanced developmental art program, these texts are designed to build upon students' learning in three major areas: creating art, looking at art, and living with art. Content and activities reflective of art production, art history, art criticism, and aesthetics are presented in a balanced and integrated manner. Students are challenged to use critical thinking in the study of artworks, artistic thinking in the creation of artworks during studio activities, and logical thinking as they learn to reflect upon and analyze what they have experienced.

CONCLUSION

Discipline-based art instruction is based upon the premise that art is a discipline comprised of four domains: art production, art history, art criticism, and aesthetics. These domains encompass conceptions about the practice and understanding of art and can guide educational practice. The intent of this chapter has been to provide suggestions for the implementation of a discipline-based approach in the teaching of art to middle school students. Art teachers can plan instruction to take advantage of the increased abilities of middle school students to create artwork, to think more abstractly and critically, and to engage in meaningful discussions while learning about art. A discipline-based art program should be an inclusive approach to the study of art, empowering students with a more sophisticated and in-depth understanding and valuing of art.

REFERENCES

Battin, M. P., Fisher, J., Moore, R., & Silvers, A. (1989). *Puzzles about art: An aesthetic casebook.* New York: St. Martin's Press.

Biehler, R. R., & Snowman, J. (1990). *Psychology applied to teaching* (6th ed.). Boston, MA: Houghton Mifflin.

Bloom, B. S., Engelhart, M. D., Furst, E. J., Hill, W. H., & Krathwohl, D. R. (Eds.). (1956). *Taxonomy of educational objectives: The classification of educational goals.Handbook I: Cognitive domain.* New York: David McKay.

Chapman, L. H. (1992a). *Art: images and ideas.* Worcester, MA: Davis Publications.

Chapman, L. H. (1992b). *A world of images.* Worcester, MA: Davis Publications.

Clark, G. A., Day, M. D., & Greer, W. D. (1987). Discipline-based art education: Becoming students of art. *Journal of Aesthetic Education, 21*(2), 130–193.

Crawford, D. W. (1987). Aesthetics in discipline-based art education. *Journal of Aesthetic Education, 21*(2), 227–239.

Dobbs, S. M. (1992). *The d.b.a.e. handbook.* Santa Monica, CA: The Getty Center For Education In The Arts.

Eccles, J. S., & Midgley, C. (1989). Stage-environment fit: Developmentally appropriate classrooms for young adolescents. In C. Ames & R. Ames (Eds.), *Research on motivation in education* (Vol. 3). New York: Academic Press.

Feldman, E. B. (1970). *Becoming human through art.* Englewood Cliffs, NJ: Prentice-Hall.

Goldstein, E., Katz, T., Kowalchuk, J., & Saunders, R. (1986). *Understanding and creating art* (Books 1 and 2). Dallas: Garrard Publishing.

Greer, W. D. (1984). Discipline-based art education: Approaching art as a subject of study. *Studies in Art Education, 25*(4), 212–218.

Hamblen, K. A. (1984). An art criticism questioning strategy within the framework of Bloom's taxonomy. *Studies in Art Education, 26*(1), 41–50.

Hillman, S. B. (1991). What developmental psychology has to say about early adolescence. *Middle School Journal, 22*(5), 3–8.

Hillman, S. B., Wood, P. C., Becker, M. J., & Altier, D. T. (1990). Young adolescent risk-taking behavior: Theory, research and implications for middle schools. In J. L. Irvin (Ed.), *Research in middle level education: Selected studies 1990.* Columbus, OH: National Middle School Association.

Hubbard, G. (1986). *Art in action* (First course and second course). San Diego, CA: Coronado Publishers.

Jackson, A. W., & Hornbeck, D. W. (1989). Educating young adolescents: Why we must restructure middle grade schools. *American Psychologist, 44*, 831–836.

Lankford, E. L. (1986). Making sense of aesthetics. *Studies in Art Education, 28*(1), 49–52.

Michael, J. A. (1983). *Art and adolescence.* New York: Teachers College Press.

Mittler, G. A. (1989). *Art in focus* (2nd ed.). Mission Hills, CA: Glencoe Publishing.

Mittler, G. A., & Howze, J. D. (1989). *Creating and understanding drawings.* Mission Hills, CA: Glencoe Publishing.

Mittler, G., & Ragans, R. (1992a). *Exploring art.* Lake Forest, IL: Glencoe.

Mittler, G., & Ragans, R. (1992b). *Understanding art.* Lake Forest, IL: Glencoe.

National Art Education Association (1972). *Art education: Middle/junior high school.* Reston, VA: National Art Education Association.

Rush, J. C. (1987). Interlocking images: The conceptual core of a discipline-based art lesson. *Studies in Art Education, 28*(4), 206–220.

Salome, R. A. (1984). A guide to critical analysis of art forms. *Viewpoints*, Fall, 11–15.

Toepher, C. F., Jr. (1990). Implementing turning points: Major issues. *Middle School Journal, 21*(5), 18–21.

"Muddling" Through the Middle School Years? An Alternative Approach Through Art

Anne G. Wolcott
Virginia Beach City Public Schools

S. Renee Miller
Sherwood Githens Middle School

Recently, the growing trend toward teaching art to children has been to include aesthetics, art criticism, art production, and art history as content for study derived from a broad range of the visual arts. The goal of contemporary art education is to enable students not only to make art but also to understand art in all its functions. The emphasis on revising the aims and objectives of teaching art has resulted in new directions and demands for developing a middle school art curriculum. This chapter presents a flexible, multiple model to effectively integrate the four disciplines of art and addresses the need to provide teachers with content as well as practical, effective strategies adaptable to the middle school art program.

INTRODUCTION

While teaching an art methods course for elementary education majors at Pennsylvania State University, we devised an instructional unit incorporating a Discipline Based Art Education (DBAE)–type approach to learning in art, interweaving studio production with art history, art criticism, and aesthetics. Our primary requirement for the unit was a strong thematic focus. We selected "the self" as an appropriate theme of importance not only for the elementary education majors in our class, but also for their future students because focus on the self is crucial throughout the educational process. The unit, taught for a semester, was a success; students learned about a variety of artists and techniques as they integrated art learning with other disciplines connecting historical information, methods of art criticism, and various philosophical approaches in art.

Since that time, we have continued experimenting with the original unit, taking it to new levels of exploration within our respective teaching areas. Since one of us has been teaching art in a middle

The middle
school curriculum
is complex, for
children at this
age level are
undergoing intense,
life—shifting
experiences.

school and the other has been directing lab experiences for university students planning to teach children in the same age range, the unit has logically evolved into a model for a middle school art curriculum. This model is especially effective because it is flexible in terms of theme, artists to be taught, content, context, scope, and sequence.

SPECIAL NEEDS OF THE MIDDLE SCHOOL STUDENT

The middle school curriculum is complex, for children at this age level are undergoing intense, life-shifting experiences. As Bracey (1993) states, "Listening to people talk about the middle school years, I often think that phase should be renamed the 'muddle school years,' with many children mired in a state of 'mental pause'" (p. 731). With the transition from elementary to middle school, students experience a radical shift in their environment which affects everything from social pressures to academic expectations. Bracey points out, "Just as these youngsters are bidding for more autonomy, the middle school controls them more; just as they are entering a period of increased self-consciousness, the middle school promotes social comparison" (p. 731).

A middle school curriculum in general must be sensitive to the needs of such a special group. "The period of transescence, or the time of transition from childhood to adolescence, is an extremely critical period in the development of an individual" (Johnson, 1992, p. 21). Contradictions characterize this stage. Pre-adolescents have a hyper-awareness of what is going on around them; yet, paradoxically, the next moment they tune everything out and become completely self-absorbed. Their minds beg for intellectual stimulation while at the same time they try to be "cool" and focus on their friends, ignoring the teacher. They want to fit in somewhere but also want to be considered unique individuals.

MIDDLE SCHOOL CURRICULUM DEVELOPMENT

Understanding the specific characteristics and needs of students is important in developing curricula for the middle school art program. To promote effective learning, a middle school curriculum must reflect the fact that "all learning involves thinking" (Chapel Hill-Carrboro City Schools, 1993, p. 5). The most recently developed curriculum (1993) for Chapel Hill-Carrboro City Schools in North Carolina outlines four primary practices and nine detailed subpractices for middle school faculty to utilize in their respective teaching domains. The four primary practices are delineated as the following:

1. Practices that foster positive attitudes and perceptions.
2. Practices that foster acquiring and integrating knowledge.
3. Practices that foster using knowledge meaningfully.

4. Practices that foster productive habits of mind.

The nine subpractices, also evident in the curriculum model, are

1. Establish a positive classroom environment where students feel accepted by their teacher(s) and classmates.
2. Develop lessons that students perceive as valuable and believe they can complete successfully. When making assignments, ensure that students fully understand the task and what is expected of them.
3. When teaching facts and concepts, help students to connect the new information to the current knowledge, organize the new information and remember it.
4. When teaching skills or processes, help students construct models of the skills or processes and perfect and internalize the skills and processes.
5. Help students extend and refine their knowledge by involving them in such activities as comparing, classifying, inducing, deducing, analyzing errors, constructing support, abstracting, and analyzing and articulating personal perspectives about issues.
6. Help students use knowledge meaningfully by involving them in application-oriented, long-term student projects that entail such activities as decision-making, investigation, experimental inquiry, problem-solving, and invention.
7. Help students self-direct thinking skills such as being aware of their own thinking and planning, being aware of necessary resources, being sensitive to feedback, and evaluating the effectiveness of their actions.
8. Help students develop critical thinking skills such as being accurate and seeking accuracy, being clear and seeking clarity, being open-minded, restraining impulsivity, taking a position when the situation warrants it, and being sensitive to the feelings and level of knowledge of others.
9. Help students develop creative thinking skills, such as engaging intensely in tasks even when answers and solutions are not immediately apparent; pushing the limits of their knowledge and abilities; generating, trusting, and maintaining their own standards of evaluation; and generating new ways of viewing a situation outside the boundaries of standard conventions. (pp. 7-22)

Understanding the specific characteristics and needs of students is important in developing curricula for the middle school art program.

In tandem with curriculum reform in education, art educators nationwide are focusing on similar goals (NAEA, 1986; Dobbs, 1992). Currently, the National Art Education Association (1993) is urging support for a "Recognizing Excellence Agenda" which outlines a vigorous program to improve performance at all levels of visual art education. The objectives of the agenda emphasize developing materials and strategies, defining curriculum content, revising pedagogy, and refining assessment. To ensure that these objectives are met, art educators must design and implement art programs at the middle school level which broaden students' understanding of art and make production more meaningful. There is also a need for flexible, multiple models providing teachers with various routes by which to develop individual curricula targeted to the school system, the school, and varying groups of students.

The art program at the middle school needs to meet a multitude of criteria. It must align itself with state mandates, system guidelines, individual school philosophies, and grade-level and interdisciplinary needs, all the while maintaining its integrity as an art program. Developing an art program at the middle school level requires not only consideration of the goals of the profession, but the special needs of the student as well (Johnson, 1992). The middle school art educator must provide opportunities for students to explore their interests; provide a broad range of exposure to works of art, media, and techniques; integrate and reinforce learning with various other disciplines in the curriculum; and remain sensitive to the physical and emotional characteristics of students just entering the throes of adolescence.

LEARNING IN ART

The flexible model unit of the middle school art curriculum presented here aims to help art teachers design and implement lessons that include art history, aesthetics, art criticism, and art production in a balanced manner. We believe students need to be challenged both intellectually and creatively in the middle school art program and that they are not only capable but are willing to deal with complex, challenging concepts and activities. Mentally stimulating and interesting contemporary avenues to art learning can easily be integrated into basic studio activities, providing an enriching, personally meaningful, and cognitively challenging educational experience.

Art production is a fundamental activity for young children, providing hands-on tasks that allow for skill building and imaginative thinking (Alexander, 1992). Current art education philosophy emphasizes the acquisition of knowledge about art that goes beyond the basic techniques of production. Such knowledge must provide both the language and the content of art: a working vocabulary for describing images as well as critical approaches and an evolving perceptual awareness that exercises reflective, critical, and analytical thinking skills. This approach must include not only studio production but also reading and writing of criticism, written and discursive analysis of works of art by students and artists, and philosophical discussion of the nature of art and the various issues surrounding art. By implementing an approach to art learning that integrates the four disciplines of art, the middle school art educator will ensure students a

The art program at the middle school needs to meet a multitude of criteria.

practical and enlightening educational experience that can connect to their life experiences.

This middle school art curriculum is addressed from the direction of content and process. This is a broader stance than that taken in years past when the primary objectives of the middle school art educator were oriented toward the creative process. However, according to Linderman (1971), even in the early seventies, art educators were interested in emphasizing art from a contemporary context. There was also a desire at the "junior high" level to use motivation "as an intellectual challenge to thought. Motivation as the sparker is intended to ignite thinking and push art learning forward" (p. 68). Such an intellectual challenge at the middle school level is not only necessary, but also desirable because students seem to crave mental stimulation whether they are aware of it or not. Middle school teachers may use different approaches at different times but should recognize that students at this juncture in their lives need to be encouraged and challenged to find and push their limits. There are many possibilities for the art educator to offer students a wide variety of experiences from the art world in the following model.

Current art education philosophy emphasizes the acquisition of knowledge about art that goes beyond the basic techniques of production.

THE UNIT

While integrating the four disciplines of art, this unit has a thematic basic structure, yet is flexible enough to incorporate multiple approaches to art learning. The thematic structure allows for interconnecting ideas not only within the art curriculum, but also with other subject areas in the general education of the adolescent. This interconnection is particularly important in a middle school curriculum which strives to promote interdisciplinary learning to foster self-expression, skills development, and social and emotional development (Johnson, 1992).

The theme provides consistency and allows the connection of concepts and multiple approaches to learning about art and artists. The theme of this unit was based on the concept of the self, offering numerous possibilities for instructional choices such as the selection of the artists and works of art for study, the issues surrounding that artist and her or his works of art, the type of content to be studied, and the discipline(s) to be emphasized.

Getting Started

Before beginning this unit, we selected an artist who had produced several self-portraits and who was featured in a video we could obtain. Copies of this artist's self-portraits, as well as a variety of self-portraits by other artists, were collected. Since this unit was designed to stimulate students to discover concepts of an artist's work using their own natural inquiry processes, it was not necessary that the featured artist be well-known.

WOLCOTT & MILLER

Talking About "The Self"

Phase one of the unit began with an introductory discussion of the concept of the self. Students were questioned about what the concept meant to them. Following the discussion, students viewed a video about an artist who discussed his art and life. Viewing the video allowed students to get to know and understand the artist through a medium other than written biography or visual works. Discussion then focused on aspects of the self that were evident in the artist's work. Questions such as, "What does the artist say?", "What do you see?", "How is this work self-referential?", and "How is this work similar, dissimilar, or both to other self-portraits?" elicited articulate responses.

The next step involved looking at selected slides of the artist's other self-portraits and discussing them using questions such as: "What is a self-portrait?", "Why do artists make self-portraits?", "What kinds of self-portraits do they make?", "What do you see in the images shown?", "What aspects of the self are conveyed?", "How are the artist's self-portraits different?", "And similar to one another?", "How are the styles similar or different?", and "What do you think is the content or meaning of these self-portraits?" The students offered insightful observations and questions about the possible meanings of the works. The students also practiced art criticism by interpreting and discussing the works on a variety of levels: describing what they saw, identifying how the artist made his work self-referential, discussing how symbolism was incorporated into the images, speculating about the artistic and literary influences that might have affected the work, determining how the work is related to other art and to the artist's own art, and formulating possible meanings of the works. For the young critics, the works of art presented somewhat familiar, yet intriguing, aspects of people's lives.

Artistic Production

The next activity in the unit was a studio project and focused on drawing a self-portrait. Students were given handouts on facial proportions and, after a brief discussion, drew classmates' portraits as a warm-up to drawing their own self-portraits. Their first self-portrait was a contour drawing which was then used as a guide for a second self-portrait created in oil pastels. The studio activity culminated in a critique. Students discussed the oil pastel self-portraits in terms of the formal elements of design and the unique styles and personal characteristics of each student-artist. Students were intrigued by one another's visual interpretations and the variety of ways in which they portrayed themselves.

Students then viewed and discussed slides of such non-traditional self-portraits as Jim Dine's *Two Robes*, Marc Chagall's *I and the Village*, Frieda Kahlo's *The Little Deer*, *The Wounded Deer*, and Rene Magritte's *The False Mirror*. Discussion focused on symbolic self-portraits and why artists would choose to create them. Questions about the power and meaning of the imagery, the relationship of symbols to experiences in the artist's life, and the methods for interpreting an artist's self-portrait as an offering of the inner self stimulated careful observations and interesting interpretations of possible meanings of the works. This discussion prepared students for the next activity: the creation of a symbolic self-portrait. Students were provided with an outline of nine questions designed to help them formulate verbal "self-portraits" of their inner selves. Questions such as, "What do you feel most passionate about and why?", "What one question would you want answered and why?", and "What is the one thing you want people to remember about you and why?" evoked thought-provoking responses. In order to establish a sense of trust and community within the class, the teacher offered her own examples for each question, thereby sharing something of herself. This appeared to stimulate honesty in the students' writings as some students delved deeply into themselves, learning more about themselves in the process.

The written symbolic self-portraits were then used as guides to create mixed-media self-portraits. Students were given the option of using pen and ink, charcoal, oil pastel, wax crayon, pencil or a combination of these to create the symbolic works. The characteristics of the various media and the choices as to which would best illustrate what they wanted to convey were discussed. Once the studio activity was completed, students presented both their written and visual self-portraits to the class. The self-portraits were displayed around the classroom while students took turns reading their essays and letting classmates guess which were their visual interpretations. Following this exchange, the teacher initiated a discussion of interpretation as both a verbal and written form. This naturally evolved into a consideration of what criticism is and what critics do, and included discussion of art critics and other types of critics as well. For the next class, students were asked to bring in various examples of written criticism about art, theater, dance, movies, or whatever they could find.

The next meeting produced a potpourri of critical articles which were compared by looking at the subject of criticism, the style of writing, the use of language, and the success of the critic in verbally reconstructing the experience or the image. At this point, students were referred back to the artist whose works and life began the unit. They were then shown a reproduction of one of this artist's works they had not seen previously. While viewing the work, students wrote a two-page criticism, beginning with descriptions and interpretations of the work, then providing reasons for their interpretations, and ending with an evaluation of whether the work was or was not of value to themselves, to the art world, and to society in general. Students discussed the writing activity and focused on how reflecting and writing on the work of art for an extended period of time gave them more opportunity to delve into possible meanings of the work as well as to discern why they responded as they did. Discussion also involved how prior knowledge of the artist and his work provided a

In order to establish a sense of trust and community within the class, the teacher offered her own examples for each question, thereby sharing something of herself.

The bookmaking project was a culmination of all that the students had learned throughout the unit.

deeper understanding of the art and possible insights into why the artist made that particular image.

At this point, some students brought up the critic's role in interpretation and how it might influence what people think. Students were asked to pursue this idea by finding an article focusing on one of the artist's works and bringing it in to share with the class. Not everyone was successful in finding information, but the majority of the students discovered good examples of writings about the artist's work. These essays and articles, dating from the 1960s to the present, gave the students an overview of many of the artist's creations. The students discussed what was communicated in the articles, how it was expressed, and in what style it was conveyed: as narrative, humor, verse, analytical description or judgment. As part of this activity, students reviewed the previously viewed slides and reproductions of the artist's works and looked for the particular works of art discussed in the criticism articles. This process led to a discussion about how contextual information can change our initial perceptions and interpretations of works of art. It took a couple of classes to thoroughly go over the articles and review the works. Most students agreed that their research had broadened their interpretations and contributed to a better understanding of the work.

Once the survey of critical methods was completed, students moved on to dealing more specifically with aesthetic issues, discussing art in a more general sense. Two approaches to aesthetics were used: (a) the philosophical discussion of aesthetic issues and (b) the application of aesthetic theory. Using specific paintings to illustrate which theories might best explain the images provided the students with better understandings of both the aesthetic theories and the works of art. By that point, they had viewed the works of various artists and one artist in-depth, read and written about the artworks, and created visual interpretations. Students were presented with the philosophical question, "Should self-portraits be representational?" This question facilitated a lively discussion in which it became pleasantly obvious that students were listening and learning from each other throughout this experience. Their responses were primarily based on what that they had read and discussed in class. Their discussion led to other aesthetic issues: "Is contextual information important in understanding art?", "Why do we have critics?", "Should we have critics?", "What function do they serve?", "What makes an artist's work art?", "Who says it is art?", "If critics say it is art and students say it is not, does that mean it is art?" and "Why or why not?" These discussions also returned to issues of criticism and interpretation, and soon it became apparent to the students that aesthetic issues and criticism overlapped.

Web-writing
Over the next few class periods, students wrote a composition using the web-writing technique described in *Writing the Natural Way* by Gabriele Rico (1983). The titles of the artist's works were written on

pieces of paper and placed in a hat. Each student then drew a title out of the hat and, using that particular title, used web-writing to create a new work. As in the case of the criticism articles, the students' writings could be narrative, descriptive, poetic, or fictional. When the students finished writing, they discussed the writings and addressed such questions as "What is the purpose of the writing?", "Why use the titles of the artist's work?", and "How does this relate to what you have been studying?" Some students pointed out that studying about an artist in this way had given them insights into themselves. They also discovered they had been learning quite a bit and were able to articulate what they had learned. Such achievements offer valuable positive reinforcement for middle school students.

Students each then made an illustration to accompany their writing. The illustration could be drawn as a serial like a comic strip or as a depiction of only one aspect of their writing. The choice of media was open. A discussion of the purpose of the illustrations led to an explanation of how they could also be incorporated into the book the students would make as their final assignment of the unit.

The bookmaking project was a culmination of all that the students had learned throughout the unit. They were shown Japanese accordion books, and the teacher demonstrated various techniques of putting the book together. The students then made their own accordion books, integrating the text of the web-writing and images from the illustrations and additional drawings, treating the book as an individual work of art. The students prepared several thumbnail sketches and decided on lettering techniques that were compatible with their imagery. After selecting key imagery and determining the text, students assembled their books. They then made decisions concerning cover illustration techniques and the color, lettering, materials, number of pages, and number of volumes necessary to complete the assignment. Once students had completed their books, a final critique offered another opportunity to share thoughts about the books and the whole experience of the unit on the self. The books, visual images, and writings were exhibited together to document the entire process of the unit. The student exhibition was offered not only as a visual experience but also as a learning experience for interested observers as well.

CONCLUSION

Art teachers in the middle school classroom can provide students with opportunities to look at, create, talk about, and write about art. This unit integrated the disciplines of art and allowed students to explore various avenues of creative and artistic expression. They learned how to negotiate interpretation verbally and visually and became aware of how artists express themselves. After several successful pilot experiences, this project is still growing and being

Art teachers in the middle school classroom can provide students with opportunities to look at, create, talk about, and write about art.

refined to include different artists and other approaches to art production, writing, and interpretation.

The development of this unit was a response to current revisions in art education content that integrate art criticism, art history, aesthetics, and art production. The success of this instructional unit confirms that the intellectual content of art study can be integrated into the middle school curriculum. This expansion of visual-art content exercises language arts skills, problem-solving skills, and critical thinking skills. Most importantly, this appraoch connects art to other avenues of knowledge and learning; thus, reciprocally, learning in art is reinforced by the skills developed within this unit.

REFERENCES

Alexander, K. (1992). Art curricula by and for art educators. In A. Johnson (Ed.) *Art education: Elementary* (pp. 1–12). Reston, VA: National Art Education Association.

Bracey, G. (1993). From normal to nerd and back again. *Phi Delta Kappan, 74*(9), 731-733.

Chapel Hill-Carrboro City School System. (1993). *Middle school curriculum of the Chapel Hill-Carrboro City Schools: Vol. 1*. Chapel Hill, NC: Author.

Dobbs, S. (1992). *The DBAE handbook: An overview of discipline-based art education*. Santa Monica, CA: The J. Paul Getty Trust.

Johnson, A. (1992). The period of transescence and its relevance for the secondary level art education program. In B. E. Little (Ed.), *Secondary art education: An anthology of issues* (pp. 21–34). Reston, VA: National Art Education Association.

Linderman, E. W. (1971). *Teaching secondary school art: Discovering art objectives, art skills, art history, art ideas*. Dubuque, IA: Wm. C. Brown.

National Art Education Association. (1986). *Purposes, principles, and standards for school art programs*. Reston, VA: Author.

National Art Education Association. (1993). *Recognizing excellence agenda briefing paper series*. Reston, VA: Author.

Rico, G. (1983). *Writing the natural way*. New York: St. Martins Press.

The Connective Power of Stories in Art

"What is usually most educationally effective is telling children good stories about their world and about the variety of human experience in it" (Egan, 1986, p. 115).

STORIES GENERATE MEANING IN ART

Alice Arnold
East Carolina University

Stories provide valuable content and meaning that can engage the imagination and help open doors to rich visual expression. At a time in their lives when many adolescents are searching for new goals (Erikson, 1968), stories offer diverse educational arenas giving students options and ideas that can be both novel and challenging. Rich stories, like good companions, acquaint students with moral questions and "help them make choices" (Coles, 1989, p. 203) that can enhance their lives.

From folktales and legends to contemporary fiction, the range of stories available for young people is tremendous and continues to expand. The quality of story illustration has never been so highly developed. Wonderful stories, beautifully illustrated, can be found in libraries and bookstores across the country[1] and can be introduced into the art room environment in a number of ways.

Stories can be used to help students understand powerful themes and imagine scenes that they can recreate in their art in personally meaningful ways. Listening to a story being told or a piece of poetry being read can help students create vivid mental images that transcend the experiences of their personal lives. These literary models also allow an escape from the rigidity of schooling and give students the freedom to think expansively and autonomously.

More specifically, stories can give students access to their emotional lives by illustrating problem-solving situations that mirror many of the dilemmas that they may encounter. At a time when young people are searching for identity, complex stories become "dramatizing devices" (Bruner, 1977, p. 82) that can provide guidance and structure. Even with careful listening, everyone "hears" a slightly different version, interpreting the stories within the context of his or her own internal dialogue.

When the dramatic structure of the tales is explored and discussed collectively, stories also foster a sense of belonging to a group. At a time when young people are often reluctant to confront the details of their own lives, stories can provide a non-threatening forum for exploration and mutual support.

In *Teaching as Story Telling* (1986), Kieran Egan stresses the importance of "how children use the most dramatic and powerful concepts to make sense of things" (p. 41) and urges teachers to ask the following questions: (a) What is most important about this topic?, (b) Why should it matter to children?, and (c) What is affectively engaging about it? Egan advocates the use of the story-form across the curriculum:

> The story is not a cultural universal for nothing. The power of good stories to engage children and stimulate their imaginations, and enlarge their experience, sympathies, and understanding, is ignored at considerable educational cost. Some parents and some teachers read stories to children every day. This seems to me to have clear educational advantages. (p. 84)

TEACHING YOUTH "AT-RISK" THROUGH STORIES

Because the youth of this country are often described as being "at-risk," all of those concerned with the future of this country must work together to strengthen the educational system that exists. The literature on middle school education of the past decade is marked with a gravity that is difficult to ignore. The titles of books and essays indicate that many educators believe the youth of this country are in peril and that the future of the country rests on its ability to marshall the talents needed to teach this age group with renewed awareness and dedication.

Growing Up Forgotten (Lipsitz, 1980), *All Grown Up and No Place to Go: Teenagers in Crisis* (Elkind, 1984), *After School: Young Adolescents on their Own* (Lipsitz, 1986), and *Turning Points: Preparing American Youth for the 21st Century* (Carnegie Council on Adolescent Development, 1989) all warn of systemic societal changes that are placing students, especially those from ages ten to fifteen, at increased risk. Isolation and undue peer pressure can foster lives marked by failure and frustration.

The Carnegie Report (1989) describes the middle grades in young people's lives as a key time of decision-making—a time when they move toward a future that will be characterized either by fulfillment and continuous self-actualization or by school failure and the inability to meet the demands of the workplace. The council reports

At a time when young people are often reluctant to confront the details of their own lives, stories can provide a non-threatening forum for exploration and mutual support.

The world is being rapidly transformed by science and technology in ways that have profound significance for our economic well-being and for a democratic society. . . . Moreover, our schools are producing all too few young adolescents with higher skill levels and problem-solving abilities that the economy increasingly needs. The time has come for a fundamental reassessment of this pivotal institution in the lives of these young people. (p. 12)

The consensus among these reports on the middle school child is that a team approach, one that places students in stronger school and community networks, should be adopted. Schools need to provide students with classes that are conducive to higher-order thinking and in which cooperation with others is the norm.

Classrooms need the kind of restructuring that will encourage communication networks to develop among students and put children's developmental needs, especially their emotional needs, at the center of concern. Dorman, Lipsitz, and Verner (1985) outline a seven-step framework for school improvement. In brief, the recommendations are as follows:

1. Diversity of the educational environment.
2. Self-exploration and self-definition.
3. Meaningful student participation in schools and communities.
4. Positive social interaction with peers and adults.
5. Physical activity that is structured, rather than ignored.
6. Competence and achievement through high-interest exploratory courses.
7. Overall structure and the establishment of clear limits. (p. 46)

Students need classes that allow them to develop and reflect on their new capacity for more abstract thought (Inhelder & Piaget, 1958). They must be allowed to address the larger questions of their lives. Dorman et al. (1985) also discuss the need for self-exploration by suggesting that students be encouraged to pursue answers to their own questions as well as those of the teachers.

Clearly, there is a need for a renewed commitment to teaching values (Kohlberg & Candee, 1984) in the schools. A recent issue of *Educational Leadership* (Brandt, 1993) is devoted to the theme of character education and offers strategies to nurture greater autonomy and self-esteem in students. Brooks and Kann (1993) also emphasize the worth of morally inspiring literature and a language-based curriculum:

> Children entering the schools today often lack the vocabulary for understanding basic value concepts such as "honesty" and "courage." Even when they can define such values, they often fail to connect

Clearly, there is a need for a renewed commitment to teaching values (Kohlberg & Candee, 1984) in the schools.

them to their own behavior. Successful character education programs focus students' attention on the basic language that expresses core concepts and links the words to explicit behavior. (p. 20)

A return to a values-based education, an education designed to develop the skills necessary for ethical decision-making, is one way to reverse some of the alarming trends that face our nation (US Department of Education, 1983). The use of literature and stories throughout the curriculum can be a vital component of a values-based education that begins to connect all of what we teach to students (Perkins, 1993).

Stories in the art classroom can be used to teach tolerance and to give students examples of the kind of moral problem-solving and decision-making skills they will need to be fully functioning and flexible adults. The following classroom scenario provides examples of ways in which a story can integrate moral problem-solving with the art-making process (Jacobs, 1989).

A FOLKTALE TO INSPIRE AND INSTRUCT:
THE GIRL WHO LOVED WILD HORSES

A university-sponsored art class, open to students from the community (ages eight through eleven) became the "practice ground" for storytelling in the art room. The university's art education students settled on the theme "Stories from Many Lands" for the fall semester; each lesson would touch on that theme by exploring ideas from a diverse culture and geographic location. For the first lesson, Paul Goble's Caldecott medal winner, a picture book called *The Girl Who Loved Wild Horses* (1978) would be the basis for a large group mural depicting a pivotal scene—a scene of drama and importance. This story, a Cheyenne tale of transformation, was chosen for its universal appeal and its authenticity in illustration of Cheyenne design.

Goble has retold over twenty Native American folktales in book form and has illustrated each with exquisite detail in pen, ink, and watercolor. The animals and people in the stories are depicted with reverence and sensitivity in harmony with each other and the land.

The young Cheyenne girl of the story has an extraordinary affinity for her tribe's horses and is able to understand them in special ways. One day, swept up in a stampede caused by a fierce thunderstorm, she rides one of the terrified horses to "hills the girl had never seen before" (Goble, 1978). The lost band joins a herd of wild horses led by a "beautiful spotted stallion," who nurtures them as they run free and wild. But the girl's people continue to search for her; in a wild chase, they capture her and take her home. As happy as she is to see her parents, she misses the wild horses, and the stallion comes each evening "neighing sadly from the hilltop above the village." She falls ill from pining, so her people allow her to return to her wild friends.

The use of literature and stories throughout the curriculum can be a vital component of a values—based education...

Each year, she returns home and brings her family a new colt. Then, one year the girl is gone—and, only a beautiful mare is seen running beside the wild stallion.

The lesson began by viewing slide images of horses and discussing the portrayal of horses in several works of art. *The Horse Fair*, a panoramic action-filled painting by Rosa Bonheur, was used to begin the discussion. Students then viewed the more colorful painting, *Blue Horses* by Franz Marc, and were asked to compare and contrast it to the Bonheur image. They then discussed the different interpretations of horses that can be found in works of art. Finally, the large bold bronze sculpture, *Horse and Rider* by Marino Marini, provided additional information that enlarged the students' "imagic store" (Broudy, 1987, p. 18) which could later manifest itself in their own art production.

The class speculated about how their feelings might change if they were able to travel to the Hirshhorn Museum and Sculpture Garden to confront Marini's large scale bronze of nearly seven feet. The discussion focused on the emotional content of the sculpture. Students were asked to think about the messages these works of art can have for the viewer and the power these images might contain. Then, the lead teacher retold the Cheyenne folktale, pausing to show the carefully rendered illustrations. Because of its dramatic content, the stampede scene was selected as the focal point for the group mural. This stormy scene would serve as the backdrop for each child's individual contribution to the mural and would help unify the colorful collage.

The lead teacher and art education students created a large black thundercloud from craft paper before the art class began. Placed on a standard size bulletin board, covered with solid orange paper, this cloud set the stage for the mural that was to unfold. Sheets of craft paper in orange, yellow, black, and red were pre-cut into smaller sections, and students could work in areas as large as they wished. Colored construction paper in many sizes and shapes was also provided.

Images of birds, cacti, horses, and tepees were suggested by the art education students, but the children also included cliffs and boulders, lightning bolts, owls, ground squirrels, and a girl on horseback, her hair flowing in the wind. The horses were created in brown, black, and black with red spots and were varied in size. They overlapped one another and flowed off the edges of the background paper. Construction paper cacti were elaborated with white chalk, and the horses were given additional definition with black felt-tip markers and white chalk.

During the lesson, an ongoing "reflective dialogue" (Taunton, 1984, p. 15) transpired between the teachers and students, promoting questions and analyses of the work in progress. The last ten minutes of class were reserved for joining the mural together with push pins and reflecting further on the students' efforts (see Figure 1). We talked about how to assemble so many pieces and whether or not the larger horses should be placed behind the smaller ones. Everyone

Middle school students need the opportunity to be involved in activities that allow them to take learning to new levels of integration and synthesis.

ARNOLD

25

Figure 1.
Class mural: The rich
visual imagery in the
finished collage was
inspired by the use
of storytelling as the
central focus of the
art activity.

became involved in these decisions and seemed
energized by the process.

Eight horses, strongly conveying the spirit of galloping, dominated
the scene. Birds flew across a large yellow sun, and brightly colored
tepees peeked out from behind the galloping herd of horses.

Throughout this process, we all learned something about life long
ago, and we learned about the mediating techniques that Native
Americans used, which lead to consensus in decision-making. As
future teachers, the art education students also gained practical experience working with a mixed-age group of young artists learning to
cooperate and work successfully with each other.

CONCLUSION

Middle school students need the opportunity to be involved in activities that allow them to take learning to new levels of integration and
synthesis. Storytelling and art-making can provide a platform for the
integration of multiple ways of knowing (Samples, 1992). By using art
and storytelling together in lessons such as the one described here,
teachers can provide a synergistic curriculum based on the developmental needs of children and, as a result, foster greater educational
progress.

NOTES

[1]Books that have specific themes can be located through the following library resources (This list is part of a more extensive bibliogra-

phy of library resources found in *Teaching With Trade Books*, K-8 by Agnes Stahlschmidt, 1989.):

Promoting World Understanding Through Literature, K-8 by Mary C. Austin and Ester C. Jenkins (1983), Libraries Unlimited, Inc. Contains an extensive bibliography of works dealing with African-Americans, Native Americans, and Hispanics.

Comics to Classics: A Parents' Guide to Books for Teens and Preteens by Arthea (Charles) Reed (1988), International Reading Association. Annotated booklist of over 300 books for young people organized by theme, with guides to appropriate age ranges.

Your Reading: A Booklist for Junior High and Middle School Students edited by Jane Christensen (1983). National Council of Teachers of English. An annotated listing of over 3,000 fiction and non-fiction titles published since 1975. Arranged by subject matter with author and title indexes. Grades 5–9.

REFERENCES

Brandt, R. S. (1993). Overview: What can we really do? *Educational Leadership, 51*(3), 5.

Brooks, B. D., & Kann, M. E. (1993). What makes character education programs work? *Educational Leadership, 51*(3), 19–21.

Broudy, H. S. (1987). *The role of imagery in learning.* Los Angeles: The Getty Center for Education in the Arts.

Bruner, J. S. (1977). *The process of education.* Cambridge, MA: Harvard University Press.

Carnegie Council on Adolescent Development: Task Force on Education of Young Adolescents. (1989). *Turning points: Preparing American youth for the 21st century.* New York: Author.

Coles, R. (1989). *The call of stories: Teaching and the moral imagination.* Boston: Houghton Miffin Company.

Dorman, G., Lipsitz, J., & Verner, P. (1985). Improving schools for young adolescents. *Educational Leadership, 43*(6), 44–49.

Egan, K. (1986). *Teaching as story telling: An alternative approach to teaching and curriculum in the elementary school.* Chicago, IL: The University of Chicago Press.

Elkind, D. (1984). *All grown up and no place to go: Teenagers in crisis.* Reading, MA: Addison-Wesley.

Erikson, E. (1968). *Identity: Youth and crisis.* New York: W. W. Norton.

Goble, P. (1978). *The girl who loved wild horses.* Scarsdale, NY: Bradbury Press.

Inhelder, B., & Piaget, J. (1958). *The growth of logical thinking from childhood to adolescence.* New York: Basic Books.

Jacobs, H. (1989). *Interdisciplinary curriculum: Design and implementation.* Alexandria, VA: Association for Supervision and Curriculum Development.

Kohlberg, L., & Candee, D. (1984). The relationship of moral judgment to moral action. In L. Kohlberg (Ed.), *Essays on moral development: Vol. 2. The psychology of moral development.* San Francisco: Harper and Row.

Lipsitz, J. (1980). *Growing up forgotten: A review of research and programs concerning early adolescence.* New Brunswick, NJ: Transaction Books, Inc.

Lipsitz, J.S. (1986). *After school: Young adolescents on their own.* Carrboro, NC: Center for Early Adolescence.

Perkins, D. (1993). The connected curriculum. *Educational Leadership, 51*(2), 90–91.

Samples, B. (1992). Using learning modalities to celebrate intelligence. *Educational Leadership, 50*(2), 62–66.

Stahlschmidt, A. D. (1989). *Teaching with trade books, K–8: Library resource materials for teachers and students.* (ERIC Document Reproduction Service No. ED 305 654) Washington, D.C.: U.S. Department of Education: Office of Educational Research and Improvement.

Taunton, M. (1984). Reflective dialogues in the art classroom: Focusing on the art process. *Art Education, 37*(1), 15–16.

U.S. Department of Education (1983). *A nation at risk: The imperative for educational reform.* Washington, D.C.: U.S. Government Printing Office.

Art as a Key Element in the Development of Understanding

Andra L. Nyman
University of Georgia

The middle school student enters the threshold of adolescence from the often protected environment of the elementary school program. The transition from childhood to adulthood involves the need for reflection on the part of middle school students to better prepare for physical, intellectual, and emotional growth. The middle school art curriculum can serve to develop middle school students' understanding of themselves and the world around them. In an increasingly global society, this outcome is of utmost importance. According to Wilson (1990);

> Experts predict that by [the year] 2000 one out of every three students enrolled in the United States will be of African, Hispanic, Asian or Native American descent (Banks & Banks, 1989; Pine & Hillard, 1990). This increase in cultural diversity is significant given that in 1990 the total non-Caucasian portion of the population of the United States—not just students in school—was slightly less than 13 percent. (p. 7)

Furthermore, by the year 2080, the Mexican-American population will comprise nearly 13% of the total United States population (Spencer, 1986). For these reasons, it is imperative that school curricula undergo radical change if schools will be prepared to successfully serve the students who will populate their classrooms during the next century.

This curricular change is also key to the success of students in art classrooms. One approach, multicultural education, can provide an avenue for transforming the programs provided at the middle grades level. According to Grant and Sleeter (1989), the term "multicultural education" is used to describe curricular and pedagogical concerns related to race, ethnicity, gender, class and exceptionality (p. 53).

The middle school art curriculum can nurture the development of an individual's awareness of other cultures and their traditions through the integration of content in art appreciation, art history, and artistic heritage.

The trend towards teaching art content of a multicultural and cross-cultural nature is becoming more widely accepted. Although recently art educators have seen an increase in available resources, the teacher education programs are only beginning to address the need for specialized coursework to prepare teachers to effectively address the many issues that arise in teaching about cultural traditions and beliefs. Throughout the 1980s, growing trends in curricular development placed the emphasis on a disciplinary approach. While that approach has merit in developing technical skills, perceptual skills, and knowledge of art historical content, the middle grades teachers must recognize the necessity for a program which emphasizes the cultivation of understanding the art of many cultures and fosters tolerance for people of other cultures. The middle school art curriculum can nurture the development of an individual's awareness of other cultures and their traditions through the integration of content in art appreciation, art history, and artistic heritage.

NURTURING UNDERSTANDING AS THE KEY

Teaching for understanding can provide a focus for defining and determining the curriculum in the art program. *Understanding*, as defined by Gardner (1993), is depends upon "having a sufficient grasp of concepts, principles, or skills so that you can bring them to bear on new problems and situations" (p. 21). McLaughlin and Talbert (1993) contend that

> . . . the vision of teaching for understanding, of students and teachers engaged in constructing new knowledge, promises the kind of learning for both teachers and students that many educators, researchers, and policymakers judge most valuable to individuals and to society. This is the kind of teaching that engages students in the problems of subject matter, in the process of asking questions and seeking answers, and in pursuing deeper understanding of their world. (p. 7)

Relating art to the whole learning of the student and making the curriculum relevant for the student should be goals of any strong art program. Optimally, the middle school curriculum should be a sequential series of learning experiences which are interrelated and interdisciplinary. Real education should be a continuum and should include the interconnection of content learned in language arts, history, social studies, and the arts.

Middle school students learn about themselves through their experiences and through interactions with their world and the people who inhabit it. They develop and test their own sets of values as they learn about the system of values and morals upon which the outside world is based (Chapman, 1978). Gardner and Boix-Mansilla (1994) identified issues forming the basis for understanding, which they grouped into the following catagories: personal identity and history; group identity; group relations; the physical world; the natural/ biological world; the world of symbols; and questions dealing with "the truth, the beautiful and the good" (p.8).

INTEGRATED LEARNING AND TEACHING FOR UNDERSTANDING

Under the middle grades concept, numerous opportunities exist for enriching the general curriculum with content and experiences in the art classroom. Art learning and skills can be integrated with and generalized to other subject matter in the middle school setting. It is important for all teachers in middle school to be aware of the objectives of the art program and specifically the levels of their students' visual, perceptual, and expressive skills. These teachers will then be able to foster further development and reinforcement of such abilities by encouraging students to use these skills in other areas of their coursework.

Art education provides the student with the opportunity to engage in the process of making and appreciating visual art. Visual art can be defined as "the expression of one's thoughts, emotions and perceptions in an organized visual form" (Michael, 1964, p. 15). Art education provides experiences for exploring the creative process and for organizing and communicating ideas and self-expression through the use of materials, processes, and tools. Perceptual development is fostered as the student is engaged in becoming aware of the visual world and the language of art.

The art curriculum provides opportunities for individual and group activities, leadership, interaction, and cooperation with others. Many chances exist for sharing ideas and for personal reflection as the students learn ways of communicating their ideas and feelings. The teacher can also relate works of art and assignments to the everyday lives of the students and to the larger community in order to encourage development of sensitivity toward the ideas and needs of others. Through the study of artists and methods of artistic inquiry, the student should learn about himself or herself and grow in the ability to view self and personal ideas objectively, as well as to view the work of peers with sensitivity and appreciation for the individuality of each person.

Arguments can be made for the importance of developing the cultural awareness of our students if we are to encourage their acceptance and appreciation of the many and varied backgrounds of the people of this nation. The study of artworks and of the cultural heritage of our own and other countries can provide the basis for development of understanding and cooperation among future generations.

The teacher's decisions concerning the inclusion of specific content can also encourage the development of an awareness of artistic

Art education provides the student with the opportunity to engage in the process of making and appreciating visual art.

heritage through exposure to the ways in which artists have reflected the human condition and the natural world in their artwork. Besides learning about techniques and the artist's use of a specific medium, students can also be taught to articulate their ideas about symbolic meanings. Dialogue about artworks can be used to teach students to "discuss levels of meaning as seen in subject matter, themes, interpretations, symbolism, and expressive content . . . non-objective and functional works in relation to the moods, feelings, and ideas they seem to invoke" (Chapman, 1978, p. 216). A strong program in art should include content ranging from artistic techniques and processes to discussion and dialogue about the meaning of art and its role in our cultural heritage.

CONCLUSIONS—A CAVEAT

Middle school students are acutely aware of the social concerns that surround them and can express their concerns and reactions to the realities of life they encounter at home, within their peer groups, and through the media and popular culture. Through careful structuring of the curriculum, the art program can provide students with opportunities to deal with the economic, political, social, and ethical issues confronting them.

It is, therefore, up to the teacher to develop a framework for learning about the art of other cultures by becoming informed in order to provide a firm grounding for informed understanding on the part of the students. Lucy Lippard (1990) states her concerns as follows:

> The boundaries being tested today by dialogue are not just "racial" and "national." They are also those of gender and class, of value and belief systems, of religion and politics. The borderlands are porous, restless, often incoherent territory, virtual minefields of unknowns for both practitioners and theoreticians. Cross-cultural, cross-class, cross-gender relations are strained, to say the least, in a country that sometimes acknowledges its overt racism and sexism, but cannot confront the underlying xenophobia—fear of the other—that causes them. Participation in the cross-cultural process, from all sides, can be painful and exhilarating. I get impatient. A friend says: remember, change is a process, not an event. (p. 6)

May art education become a key part of the process of developing greater cultural understanding as we work together to make this world a better place.

REFERENCES

Banks, J. A., & Banks, C. A. (Eds.). (1989). *Multicultural education: Issues and perspectives*. Boston: Allyn and Bacon.

Through careful structuring of the curriculum, the art program can provide students with opportunities to deal with the economic, political, social, and ethical issues confronting them.

Chapman, L. H. (1978). *Approaches to art in education.* New York: Harcourt Brace Jovanovich, Inc.

Gardner, H. (1993). Educating for understanding. *The American School Board Journal, 180*(70), 21–24.

Gardner, H., & Boix-Mansilla, V. (1994). Teaching for understanding in the disciplines . . . and beyond. *Teachers College Record, 96* (2), 198–218.

Grant, C. A., & Sleeter, C. E. (1989). Race, class, gender, exceptionality, and educational reform. In J. A. Banks & C. A. M. Banks (Eds), *Multicultural education: Issues and perspectives* (pp.49–65). Boston: Allyn and Bacon.

Lippard, L. R. (1990). *Mixed blessings: New art in a multicultural America.* New York: Pantheon Books.

McLaughlin, M. W. & Talbert, J. E. (1993). Introduction: New visions in teaching. In D. K. Cohen (Ed.), *Teaching for understanding: Challenges for policy and practice.* San Francisco: Jossey Bass.

Michael, J. A. (1964). *Art education in the junior high school.* Reston: National Art Education Association.

Pine, G. J., & Hillard, A. G. (1990). Rx for racism: Imperatives for America's schools. *Phi Delta Kappan, 71*, 593–600.

Spencer, G. (1986). *Projections of the Hispanic population: 1983 to 2080* (Series p-25, No. 995). Washington, D.C.: Department of Commerce, Bureau of the Census (Eric Document Reproduction Series No. ED 301 396).

Wilson, R. (1990). The implications of changing demographics for school systems. *Education Journal, 20*(2), 3–6.

A Participant Observation Study of How a Middle School Art Teacher Integrates Multicultural Art History With Art Making

This study describes, analyzes, and interprets through participant observation how one middle school art teacher in the Southwestern United States integrates multicultural art history in his daily studio teaching. This chapter presents different content and motivation techniques and focuses on one five-week unit on teaching mask-making to one class of seventh graders, many of whom are slow learners and are from diverse cultural backgrounds. Included are recommendations for integrating art history and studio. Emphasis is on cultural understanding and ritual.

Mary Stokrocki
Arizona State University

PROBLEM AND BACKGROUND

The dominant teaching approach at the middle school level seems to be studio explorations in several media. Although in the past, art teachers at the middle school level were reluctant to teach art appreciation or art history, outside of references to a few major artworks, many art teachers are trying now to include these areas more substantially in their art programs. Day (1969) reported successful experimental results of teaching Cubism to preadolescents. Marjorie Wilson (1984) described how art teachers Jan Plank and Elizabeth Katz succeeded in teaching art history to middle school students in Ohio. In their case, selected and gifted students responded to artworks. Both of these studies were affiliated with a university or department of education, and the students were from middle- to high-income families.

Participant observation research in other settings reveals different information. After surveying secondary art teachers in Nebraska, Galbraith and Spomer (1986) found that the majority of art teachers informally connect art history to studio activities. In one of my earlier studies, I noted that art teachers at the middle/junior high level infrequently used art appreciation (Stokrocki, 1990). Students in many of these sites have had no formal elementary art experience at all. More specifically, I discovered that middle school students may respond to some art appreciation explorations of non-conventional art forms, such as photography or fashion design. In a few sites, however, students resisted reading art appreciation-oriented publications, designed for their age group. Middle school teachers frequently tell me that their main concern is to build students' confidence through visual expression and to keep students from dropping out of school. Hence, the teaching of art history or art appreciation occurs in very small doses.

In a recent examination of middle school art curricula in Ohio, Anglin (1993) found that art appreciation, as well as art history, appeared infrequently. She discovered the following mentioned categories: teaching art history periods, art in society, and architecture. With such overwhelming doubts from middle school teachers and negative attitudes from students, how can a middle school art teacher integrate the teaching of art history and art studio so that all students become more active learners?

PARTICIPANT OBSERVATION

This participant observation study began with data gathering through daily photographic, audio, and video note-taking and informal interviewing. Content and comparative analysis followed. Through content analysis of the data collected daily, I discovered repeated conceptual themes, such as the importance of humor and exaggerated stories for middle school students. Through comparative analysis, I interrelated these themes, gathered over a period of five weeks. Later, I correlated other studies with my findings to form recommendations on the integration of art history into the curriculum. At various stages of the study, the instructor clarified his behaviors and beliefs. Several interested middle school students acted as key informants (giving me additional information when needed), and two graduate students offered additional insights. Observations and interpretations of the data by the instructor's colleagues and art education reviewers enriched the total meaning of the study.

WHAT IS ART HISTORY TEACHING?

Many art teachers view art history as simply looking at artworks or, at best, teaching art appreciation. Some instructors teach art history as the transferral of information from themselves to their students. Few teachers regard art history as inquiry that is replicative or generative. Replicative inquiry allows students to discover what art historians know while generative inquiry seeks to build new information (Addiss & Erickson, 1993). Erickson believes that adolescents can begin to understand "that lifestyles, values, and beliefs have varied in different times and places" (p. 143), and she challenges teachers to make information comprehensible. So how does a middle school art teacher introduce art history for the first time?

CONTEXT

Located in a suburban university town, the observed middle school classroom had stimulating studio and art history instructional resources as well as students' artwork on display. One display, for example, featured the local Yaqui Indian culture and its masks. Ceiling posters of popular artists and idols covered the fluorescent bulbs. The art room had a television monitor and a computer. Although crowded, the room was "a cheerful atmosphere" (Wells, 1992). The instructor found his resources satisfactory, although his room was undergoing remodeling at the time of the study. The setting, therefore, was occasionally chaotic. Observations totaled 37 hours (25 visits of 1½ hours throughout 1992 and 1993.[1])

PARTICIPANTS

Formerly a performance artist and owner of a graphic arts business, the observed instructor, hereafter referred to as W, had a BFA in printmaking and photography and had taught for four years in this school. His former cooperating teacher, the district elementary art supervisor, and several of my students who had observed his teaching recommended him "as a real character." He gained support for the art program by attending school board meetings, participating in school events, and arranging art displays and shows.

The observed class of 26 students was the smallest of W's classes. In this class, over half of the students were Yaqui, a mixture of Mexican, Catholic, and Indian traditions. Many of the students were classified as slow learners,[2] two students were from PALS,[3] and all students' attitudes towards art were fairly limited[4] as this school system does not offer art at the elementary level. The students' affection for their art teacher was genuine and deepened as the course progressed due to his constant help, willingness to review, and outstanding sense of humor.

MIDDLE SCHOOL ART PROGRAM

The art program in this middle school was a popular elective and consisted of exploratory experiences of basic art elements, principles, and skills. Art units included: drawing (contour, scratchboard, and tonal completion), mola positive/negative collage, mask-making, and clay slab and pinch pots. Art appreciation accompanied every unit:

Renaissance artists and expressive lines, Mesopotamian monsters, Panama Cunan molas, cave art, masks from four cultures, and clay and the Mound Builders.

OBSERVATIONS

Overview of activities—tribal design and mask-making:

W had no written objectives for this lesson but provided an array of handouts. Featured on one mask-making handout was the function of masks, "to transform the wearer . . . to combine human and animal spirit to give the wearer super powers. American Indians use masks for religious and ceremonial purposes. . . . Masks will always remain an expression of the human spirit." Another handout featured the word *unification* which implied an integrated life and design system. Throughout the unit, W emphasized similarities and differences between life and art, then and now, and between cultures.

The lessons proceeded as follows: (a) The mask making unit began with a short story of cave life and art was designed to show how masks were part of total life. (b) Through an introduction video, W compared different cultural ideas on death with the local Day of the Dead celebration. (The Day of the Dead is a festive Mexican celebration [November 1 and 2] in memory of all the departed. Mexicans regard death as a natural cycle. They clean and decorate cemeteries with crosses, lights, and flowers, and place food and incense on the graves. Many crafts and food with the skeleton theme appear at this festival [Pomar, 1987].) (c) W introduced the studio project on mask-making with handouts to direct attention to the design principles of symmetry and repetition of art elements—shape, color, and line. He emphasized that such concepts were similar in all tribal cultures. (d) On four different days, W motivated students to plan different design solutions, utilizing excerpts from *Tribal Design* (Crizmac, 1988) videos and featuring pre-Columbian, Eskimo, and Sepik (New Guinea) masks. (e) The following week, a class demonstration of plaster modeling over a face was presented and repeated with individual groups for several days. (f) W then suggested how to form and add mask attachments. (g) Students were directed as to how to carefully prepare a mask surface and paint it. (h) Throughout the painting sessions, W reviewed and prompted students on tribal styles and life differences. (i) Finally, he gave students a written self-evaluation to complete, then followed up with short individual conferences.

Exaggerated art history stories, gradual introduction of art history, and grotesque descriptions as attention tools:

W began the unit with exaggerated art history short stories that were full of action. He believed that art history should be gradually introduced. In one lesson on cave painting, he described animal and human behavior. He began, "If a 800-pound bear is chasing you, you're in trouble. I hope that you can run fast." Then he explained how cave people used all animal parts: antlers as spear points, bones as buttons and chalk, intestine skin as water containers, skins as clothes, teeth as ornaments, and even, jokingly, "a tasty brain sandwich." Then he explained about bone marrow, "The marrow—the stuff inside of your bones—is very high in protein. They would smash the bones to get at it. It was kind of like the ice cream of the cavemen days. Marrow was mmm-mmm-good!" At this point the students were gagging, "Gross," "Yuck," "No way!" He also told students how fashionable body piercing was then and now (Wells, 1992). W used grotesque descriptions for the enhancement of memory. He played a comparative video on Aborigine masks that students listened to while working. While historical facts may have been stretched, W succeeded in capturing the students' attention.

Introduction of the mask unit and comparison of different cultural ideas and practices on death:

On the next day, W compared the local Day of the Dead ceremonies with Halloween, Yaqui-culture practices, and views on death in other cultures. W was determined to broaden his students' appreciation for other cultures' attitudes about death and to widen their conceptual basis for mask making. He believed that without the historical perspective, teaching was all craft. Towards the end of the term, W began a five-week unit on mask-making. He began his motivation:

> We're going to study masks. We all grew up with masks, especially around Halloween. They were feared—like the skeleton. Some of them were friendly, like Casper the Ghost. We're going to learn about the *Dia de los Muertos*—Day of the Dead . . . . Different cultures teach us new ideas about death. I'll show you a place in the USA where women bring notes to their dead husbands.

W then questioned his Yaqui students about their cultural knowledge. He asked, "What do the Yaqui do at the grave sites?" Students answered, "Clean them up, paint and decorate them." A brief discussion followed. He then showed students an example of the Pascal mask from Guadalupe and a *diablo* mask from Michoacán Mexico (Toor, 1985). Both masks hang on his wall. Not all of his Yaqui students were aware of the significance of their rituals.[5]

W then played another video *Death—The Trip of a Lifetime*. The narrator began, "Death is inevitable . . . . In every culture, people look beyond and see something like this romantic version" (from Jean Cocteau's famous last scene of beauty and beast rising in the clouds). Other examples included clips of a death ceremony called St. Patrice in Wales, a Zen Buddhist graveyard and bone festival, Japan's Ghost Festival and Parade in Kyoto, and Ghana's death ritual that ends with the sacrifice and consummation of a goat. The video ended with the ritualistic collection of objects (notes, a beer, flowers) that people leave at the Vietnam Memorial in a special collection in Washington, D.C. The cross-cultural comparison of views on death held students in quiet awe. They loved the fireworks at the Japanese Ghost Festival; for example, one student exclaimed, "Wow! Look at those colors!"

Day of the Dead celebration video and art forms:

Finally, W showed a video segment of the Day of the Dead (DoD) ceremony from the Heard Museum featuring the giant masks and band of the Mexican artist Zarco. W invited students to accompany him to the DoD celebration at the Heard Museum the following Saturday. He announced that he had extra funds from sponsors if their families couldn't afford the fee. Six students accompanied him to the Saturday event. W also shared some of his DoD children's toys: sugar candy skulls, an angel, and a skeleton in a box.

Several step-by-step worksheets and oral prompts to key concepts:

The next day, W reviewed the mask-making project with planning sketches and steps: an oval pattern for size, the pencil decorated version, and the colored blueprint. Besides the procedure worksheets, which he often read aloud, W prompted students' attention to key concepts during studio class. He used exaggerated sounds ("Whoa!" "Whoop!" or "Wail!") to direct their attention to such art terms as *symmetry, shape,* and *repetition.* He limited color choice to three colors and asked students to use different lines in a repetitive fashion. Finally, he reminded students to work slowly; he emphasized good craftsmanship; and he told them that their plans were worth 30% of the total mask project. Then W distributed specific directions on a worksheet:

> Design a mask on the worksheet (oval pattern). Make it original by using design elements in different ways. Make four designs based on the cultures studied. You may use any media to decorate the mask. Some possibilities are tempera, acrylics, cut paper, yarn, glitter, ribbons, feathers, and so forth.

Tribal design videos to develop cultural understanding and to generate ideas:

To promote cultural awareness and to get students to plan several mask designs beyond the typical Halloween types, W showed five-minute excerpts from three *Tribal Design* (Crizmac, 1988) videos. He announced that the basic concept was "that tribal art can teach you something about how people relate to masks." On the next day, W announced at the end of his motivation, "This art class is not about making things, but about understanding things—history, materials, form. If all you want to do is make things, you've got the wrong class" (LaPorte, 1993). Then W showed five minutes of the video on pre-Columbian art (Crizmac, 1988).

Three days later, W discussed video excerpts on pre-Columbian art as follows:

> W asked, "Where did people who inhabited South America come from?" Student 1 (S1) replied, "Mexico?" W inquired again, "Before that?" Students had no answer. W informed them that several cultures preceded the modern Mexicans, notably the Aztecs. Then he posed sideways to show what pre-Columbian Aztecs looked like—how they pushed their infants heads into "a triangular, sexy, flat-head look." Students laughed. W continued, "The climate was very warm, like here."

W later announced that they were to make mask designs derived from three cultures—New Guinea, Eskimo, and Aztec. He told students that he wouldn't accept the first ideas that they drew but would allow them to design their own later. W commented, "It's hard for kids to understand that I won't accept [just] any design. They want me to say 'That's great!' I need to see them plan a variety of designs."

Art history motivation occasionally unsuccessful due to constant interruptions and boring videos, but more successful with teacher's playful interpretative performance:
W was not always successful with art history. Students had difficulty retaining concepts because of constant interruptions, such as assemblies and field trips. During the five-week unit, five field trips occurred in seven days, and students lacked time to finish their designs. These conditions made teaching difficult, and discipline problems ensued.

In spite of these conditions, W pursued his motivation. During one video, students became fidgety and began to fool around. W stopped the video and invited one talkative student, "OK, come up and teach the class. Tell us about this culture's art (pause). You really don't know." He therefore warned the class, "We can sit and talk forever. How many of you want to make a mask? Are you with me? I know that this gets boring, but these facts are important" (five-minute interruption). The bell rang, and W ran out of time. My graduate student observer noticed that students didn't pay attention to the video (LaPorte, 1993); however, when W interpreted the facts, the students seemed more alert to the content because of his performance style.

Similarities and differences emphasized through audio-visual teaching, talk-show host style, fast pacing, and comparison with popular videos:

W catered to students' interests and multiple ways of learning through the audio-visual MTV culture by integrating such audio-visual media as music, video, and slides. His anecdotes and fast talk imitated the television program *Saturday Night Live* with such expressions as "Yo!" to redirect student attention. He showed students a five-minute excerpt, featuring changing face parts, from the Godley and Cream music video *Changing Faces* (1987). He encouraged comparisons:

> Notice the similarities as well as the differences. In our culture, it is very acceptable to wear make-up. Now in other cultures, they tattoo their faces and pierce parts of their body. If someone walked into class, people would go, "Hey, nice earrings." So, when you look at this stuff from New Guinea, don't think that it's as strange as your original reaction.

W later joked about the long hair he had earlier, but cut off to use on his own mask. Then he playfully suggested that students cut off some of the girls' hair for their own masks. "He's like a wacky professor because of his funky clothes," described one observer (Wells, 1992). On this occasion, he wore baggy army fatigues and a T-shirt that was designed with laughing skulls to commemorate the Day of Dead celebration (see Figure 1). W thus assumed multiple roles and became an entertainer. As an entertainer, he frequently talked at a fast pace. He explained, "If I don't do a lot of fast stuff, they get bored."

Student confusion over oval, overlapping, and combining forms:

Initially, several students experienced technical problems with drawing an oval shape (LaPorte, 1993). W then developed an oval pattern in the size of their face for them. Several students were also confused about how to combine human and animal forms. They placed their animal at the top of the human head, not overlapping it. The dialogue follows:

W assisted a student (S1), "Start with an oval. If you add a tail on one side, and the mask must be symmetrical, what do you add on the otherside?" S1 guessed, "Another tail?" W suggested, "OK, or a feather or a hand." W asked a second student (S2), "What animal are you making?" S2 answered, "Not sure what you mean?" W then gave an example, "Give me an animal name." S2 responded, "Bull." W demonstrated how to use a human nose instead of a bull's snout.

Other students drew a human head sitting on top of the animal's head. W constantly demonstrated individually. Later, he realized that a class demonstration would have helped.

Constant concept repetition:

Throughout every class, W constantly repeated essential concepts emphasizing studio techniques and art elements and principles (Arizona Essential Skills, 1988). Dominant art concepts included line, shape, contrast, color, and texture. W also directed students' technical awareness. On one occasion, a student who was painting his mask complained, "I can't make this nose to look the same on both sides." W responded, "That's because there's a bump. Just draw it wider down here, to make it even—symmetrical." To a second student, W added, "Remember to repeat a color which you already used over here." The term *repetition* itself became a design refrain throughout the class. He also formally quizzed students on the vocabulary and key concepts in his lessons.

Assessment as ritual identification of culture and stylistic recognition in masks:

A ritual may be considered as a prescribed form or a detailed procedure faithfully and repeatedly executed. W didn't allow students to step over the threshold of the crafts room until they had four designs, based on the four studied cultures, and could identify the stylistic aspects. W derived this type of ritualistic indoctrination and forced review from Turner's (1969) accounts of the rites of passage practiced in different cultures. During such rites of passage, tribal elders isolate initiates into a group (the rite of separation) and indoctrinate them (the rite of transi-

Figure 1. The instructor was a humorous character who wore baggy army fatigues and a T-shirt designed with laughing skulls to commemorate the Day of the Dead Celebration.

tion). After initiates have learned the sacred rites and passed the painful tests, tribal leaders allow the initiates to step into a place a honor or adulthood (the rite of integration). W mimicked these rites with humorous threats, such as Chinese torture. The next day, W prompted students to choose their best design. Examples follow:

> W to student (S), "Show me your mask plans from four cultures. Which one is Eskimo—part human and animal?" S, "This one that has teeth and ears." W, "Which one is Sepik Indian—symmetrical or even-designed?" S, "This one." W, "Good, which one is Aztec—with earrings?" W, "Which one do you want to make? Why?" S, "I like this one because of the strange shape" [It's ambiguous]. W, "Doesn't it work better when we have a good design? Excellent choice!" (see Figure 2).

> While W graded the mask designs, he strolled around to individual students and asked questions; for example, "What are the identifying features of pre-Columbian art [Aztec]? What did they do with the cradle boards?" S, "[They] smashed their heads." W, "Which made their heads and their masks look what shape?" S, "Flat." W, "What's another identifying feature?" S, "Hoop earrings." (LaPorte, 1993)

This persistent review continued throughout the studio process and into the final grading.

Figure 2. The instructor directed students individually to identify the cultural styles of their four mask designs and to give appropriate reasons for selecting the one they chose to make into a 3-D mask.

Individual and small group studio demonstration and in-process appraisal of plaster modeling process:

W began by reviewing the process of modeling plaster masks. He showed students how to (a) wrap plastic around the head, (b) insert a straw in the mouth for breathing purposes, (c) cut and dip plaster strips into water, (d) apply the strips in a criss-cross fashion, and finally, (e) smooth the plaster. Then he divided the class into groups. A small group of students cut strips of plaster at one table, while four other groups began to drape plaster strips over the plastic on the faces of teammates. Throughout the class, W reminded students to reinforce the chin area and the sides of the mask. He constantly directed individuals, "Bring plaster across [the face] in another direction to reinforce sides." Then he reminded, "Pet it [the mask], and this brings plaster to the surface. Drape plaster around the edge [of the mask] to strengthen it." He also helped students to attach appendages to their masks (see Figure 3).

Sense of humor alleviates students' fear and embarrassment:

W frequently joked with students during the plaster wrapping and modeling session. He teased a new student, "This is what we do to a new student on the first day. Welcome aboard. Breathe through the straw," as he plopped one in her mouth. He told a second group to grab a corner of the plastic to straighten it out and teased, "This is the new look this year—plaster in ear and hair." Later, he explained, "Notice that it gets warmer inside. Soon your eyebrows will ignite." Finally, he

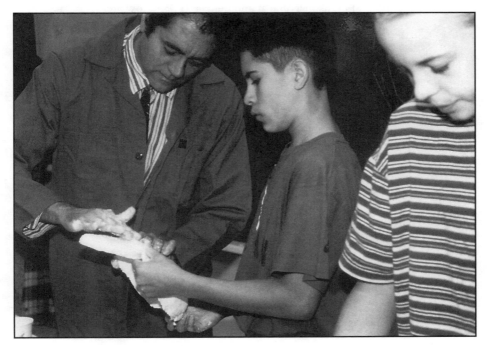

Figure 3. The instructor helped students attach appendages to their masks. He reminded them to reinforce facial additions with plaster strips applied in the opposite direction for added strength.

STOKROCKI

reminded students to wait 15 minutes for the mask to set before removing it. He realized that students were afraid and embarrassed by being temporarily disabled. W helped students relax with his sense of humor. Students enjoyed the joking. One student commented, "He understands us."

Students challenged with professional studio skills:

During an entire class period, students sanded, primed, and dried their masks with a hair dryer. They were very involved. A few students included attachments, such as clay noses or cutout styrofoam horns, covered with plaster. Two students worked on one mask; one identified the design as Eskimo because it was part animal and human. I asked him how he made the appendages, and he replied, "Roll the newspaper, cover with plaster, attach it, put on more plaster, smooth." I asked other students why they were priming their masks, and they unanimously cried, "Seal it, so it won't crack!"

Problem-solving and essential concepts learned:

Evidence from the video recording revealed that students carefully solved problems and learned essential art and cultural concepts. Photographs revealed how carefully they worked. They painted their masks in tempera and acrylic. (Example dialogue from video follows: OS = Observer Stokrocki, AF = Anglo female, AM = Anglo male, YF = Yaqui female, YM = Yaqui male.)

OS, "What culture is yours from?" AF1, "Eskimo." OS, "Why?" AF1, "Its half animal and human." OS, "How are you going to make those [seal] appendages?" AF1, "I'll use cardboard and stuff." OS, "How are you painting it?" AF1 holds up her mask and exclaims, "Outlining parts and filling them in. It will look better when it's finished." (see Figure 4)

AM draws an intricate design on mask. OS, "What kind of mask are you making?" AM, "My own design." OS, "Based on which culture?" AM, "Sepik Indians—pattern repeats itself. It's symmetrical." OS, "What does that mean?" AM, "Equal on both sides." OS, "Do you like making masks?" AM, "It's fun."

OS, "What culture is yours based on?" AF2 "Sepik Indians," OS, "Why?" AF2, "I like design and repeating patterns." OS, "That's one nifty design! How is it arranged?" AF2 turns around her mask and identifies the top. OS, "Is it symmetrical or assymetrical?" AF2, "Symmetrical." OS, "Why?" AF2, "Same on both sides." OS, "What did you learn about masks?" AF2, "It's

Figure 4. One student painted an Eskimo style mask with animal and human features by outlining parts and filling them in.

not as easy as I thought." OS, "What technique did you use? What do you call this stuff you are using?" AF2, "Plaster." OS, "How did you do it?" AF2, "Wet plaster, stick it on, sand it. When it's dry, paint it."

W was pleased that the students realized that strength lies in stylistic knowledge rather than simply process. He clarified:

> The very first week I had them draw a mask and kept those drawings to see how their designs progressed. Most of these are not their own [stereotyped] designs, but they picked a design based on tribal art. Even those that used their own designs used symmetry and repetition of simplified shapes. (LaPorte, 1993)

Ritualistic knowledge—painting secrets and technique persistence:

At times W shared ritualistic knowledge, what he called "magical secrets of the trade." On one occasion, he told students that he would show them a trick. He whispered, "Outline colors in black to make them stand out or in white to make colors recede." W appraised a student's mask, "Make [painted] lines straighter. You have hard-edged lines here. Intensify the colors by surrounding them with black. Outline with a small brush. Paint the colors again." To another student, he suggested, "This shark shape is all white now. It doesn't have a mouth, so draw it in black." (see Figure 5). She asked if she should paint the

STOKROCKI

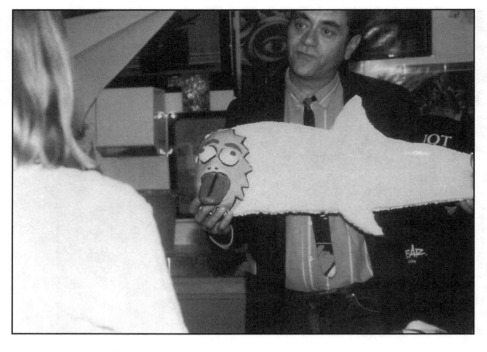

Figure 5. The instructor related "a magical secret" of the trade, "Outline colors in black to make them stand out or in white to make colors recede. This shark shape is all white now. It doesn't have a mouth, so draw it in black."

whole thing, and he answered, "Why not?" To a shy student, he praised, "Remember when you first came to art class and felt that you couldn't do anything? Sometimes 'hanging in there' and doing it over really pays. I'm proud of you. We're going to show the whole school your work." W makes persistence "a

Figure 6. Students favored the Sepik mask style of symmetry and repetition of shape: curved lines, arcs, triangles, crescents, teardrops, circles, and even this example of spiral or concentric circles within the mouth.

secret knowledge" that students learn through trial and error.

Repetition favored by students:

Most students chose to imitate the Sepik mask style and recognized the symmetrical design and repetition of pattern. The designs were carefully planned, intricate, and painted on a white background. I noted evidence of masks with curved lines, arcs, triangles, crescents, teardrops, circles, and even one example of concentric circles within the mouth (see Figure 6). One of the girls named the repeated colors and shapes that she used in her mask (see Figure 7).

The success of written self-evaluation sheets:

According to an observer (Wells, 1992), students felt uncomfortable the previous year with art critiques in front of their classmates. Private writing has worked better for them (also discovered in Stokrocki, 1990). One student commented that she "was so scared to have to talk about her mask in front of others." This year, W gave students a self-evaluation worksheet to complete. Since this was their first critique or self-evaluation, he explained the task parts. He directed students to indicate the number of points they deserved on such criteria as use of time, craftsmanship, completion, concept (clarity), and creativity (originality). W then asked a second student to grade the mask, and finally, added his own evaluation. On the back of the sheet, he asked students to identify their strengths and weaknesses and how they would improve their masks. W circulated among students and helped them with the questions. He insisted that they add what they learned (about plaster, painting, culture).

Students' responses were honest in the written evaluations that masks were harder to make then they realized, that the paint cracked, that the mask was too heavy, or that the sides were weak. Several students believed that their plans looked better because they couldn't "paint good." One student added nails as a decoration on her robot mask, after W drilled holes for her. She thought that her idea was good but that the nails made the mask weak and the sides crack. One student remembered a

Figure 7. One female student proudly named the repeated colors and shapes that she used in her mask.

culture called Yam (Sepik), and "the guy with the earrings" (Aztec) from *Tribal Design* (Crizmac, 1988) videos. One Yaqui student was extremely pleased that his mask was based on his own culture.

The attraction of Yaqui students to Mexican-culture themes and requests for more time for studio work:

Throughout the lesson, the Yaqui students quietly listened to the videos and short lectures. A group of Yaqui male (YM) students were attracted to the Mexican themes, such as the Day of the Dead *diablo* (devil)[5] , clown, and animal masks. These students found the "stuck-out" *diablo* tongue intriguing, and four students imitated it. YM1 imitated the three-dimensional *diablo* example on the wall. YM2 painted a spider web on one side of his mask and the spider on the other side (see Figure 8). YM3 painted a clown design. Clown designs are important in the Dance of Conquest of Teotitlan del Valle, Oaxaca (Toor, 1985). This student wrote, "I don't like how the colors were put on. I learned about Inters [sic]. I would put on beter colars [sic] and put on ears and horns (if I had more time)."

The Yaqui females (YF) seemed to experiment more. YF1 finished her "boar" mask with an opalescent gold acrylic over the white background; the boar image is from the Yaqui Easter ceremony. She thought that her strengths were the "top and sides of head and colors, but colors didn't come out good. Guaze [sic] was bad." Such Mexican animal masks come from the State of

Figure 8. Yaqui male students imitate Mexican style masks: a *diablo* form with human and animal characteristics.

Guerrero. YF2 used glitter paint in blue and red on her Sepik repeat-design mask. Two other YF students painted a mask together "to catch up." One painted radial patterns in the eyes and whiskers on her purple mask. She commented, "I just thought of it!" The Yaqui students found the project was fun, but they needed more time to paint their masks.

Attitude changes about art:
Students undoubtedly changed their attitudes about art from this long and involved project. One student summarized the experience well:

> I came into class not wanting to because I kept on telling myself I can't draw. I learned [art] is not just drawing. I think that the four drawings did help give me ideas [importance of planning]. I think the feathers added a lot to the mask. The mask looked bare without it. I didn't make lines as straight as I wanted it [craftsmanship]. I like the little hearts I added inside the mask's eyes.

CONCLUSIONS

This study does not prescribe that every teacher instruct in this way but presents content and methods that appear to be successful, although not perfect. Results suggest that a middle school art teacher can integrate art history and studio primarily through storytelling and teaching basic facts and description (Addiss & Erickson, 1993). Although the instructor presented exaggerated stories about several cultures, he constantly repeated formalistic, stylistic facts—the repetition of art elements and symmetry. These findings support Galbraith and Spomer's (1986) finding that art teachers may still be more concerned about teaching formal aspects of art in an informal atmosphere. On the other hand, an emphasis on cultural understanding can suggest much more—even ideas about death—existential concerns, of which students are beginning to become intensely curious. At times, however, "teacher talk" may be too one-sided (Alexander, 1977), and more effort to generate student response is needed. Constant interruptions and students' ability differences and impatience may be inhibiting factors.

Evidence suggests that slow learners may understand basic art history and cultural knowledge as a result of the constant repetition of concepts and multi-modal stimulants. This understanding includes mostly stylistic characteristics and anthropological ideas about the use of art as well as death practices in different cultures (Addiss & Erickson, 1993). Students also learned that they can get ideas for designs or art making from art history. Yaqui students in particular seem attracted to Mexican (*diablo*, animal) themes.

This study does not prescribe that every teacher instruct in this way but presents content and methods that appear to be successful, although not perfect.

The transfer of design and theme information suggests some integration between art history and studio. Initially, students may be confused by such terms as *oval, overlapping,* and *combining forms.* They seem to prefer repetition of forms and intricate patterns in their masks, as in Sepik culture design, probably because repetition is easier and is aesthetically pleasing. Zurmuehlen (1983) has suggested that repetition can be considered "the most rudimentary aesthetic [and artistic] structure" (p. 117). Only a few advanced students may accept the challenge of combining more complicated animal/human forms with an instructor's help and after school hours.[6] Although some mask decoration may not be as finished as students hoped, importance is attached to the process. Students learned as indicated on the self-evaluation sheets: that masks are not as easy to make as originally thought and require planning and persistence; craftsmanship is important as indicated in the improvements they would make on their masks; and art is much more than drawing, reflecting an attitude change. Cultural understanding, however, is difficult to determine at this stage, and evidence of such learning may appear in later years. Nevertheless, students were interested in the cultural discussions introduced by the teacher and implemented the themes and designs associated with those cultures into their own masks.

RECOMMENDATIONS

The following recommendations for integrating art history with studio at the middle school level are suggested: (a) Begin instruction with a few informal and expressive art concepts and motivational techniques related to everyday life, such as the way W related the cave people eating bone marrow to eating ice cream. (b) Compare the art of the geographic region being studied to that of similar regions, such as the Yaqui to other desert cultures. (c) Contrast cultural themes and habits of the present with the past, such as relating gangs or battle history.[7] (d) Entice students with popular cultural references to contemporary heroes or pop stars. (e) Use exaggerated stories to capture students' attention and to ease them into the study of art history. Addiss and Erickson (1993) argue for the narrative as a significant teaching structure because art history is a factual story. (f) Compare food, fashion, animals, entertainment (such as wrestling), and holidays (such as Halloween and the Day of the Dead ceremonies) between cultures. (If discussion of such practices are restricted by school policy or community values, use objective motivations such as anthropological videos comparing cultural practices.) Remember that the key concept is cultural understanding. (g) Convey stylistic concepts such as repetition of shape, pattern, color, and the combination of human and animal forms. (h) Share art historical information such as death and puberty rites as ritual secrets.[8] (i) Intersperse these motivations throughout the unit.

Communicating art historical information can be equally fascinating: (a) Use multi-modal teaching—stories, music, short video clips, popular art forms (e.g. tatoos)—and three-dimensional examples. (b) Adopt such multiple roles as cook, detective, talk show host, or anthropologist. (c) Because most students can track information quickly nowadays, consider using faster pacing and constant review as you make transitions from one theme to another. (d) Design media-oriented reviews, such as trivia contests or talk shows, to challenge student recall and understanding. Implementing art history may be occasionally unsuccessful due to interruptions, such as W experienced, and to videos that fail to interest the students, but can be more successful with a teacher's playful interpretative performance.

Studio success may be accomplished through the following: (a) Using several, step-by-step skill worksheets and demonstrations. (b) Encouraging students throughout the lesson to generate different design ideas by offering several models: art reproductions, three-dimensional folk art examples, and short video excerpts. (c) Challenging students to work individually and in groups with professional studio techniques, such as plaster modeling and surface preparation. (d) Giving constant in-process appraisal of studio technique fused with concept repetition of stylistic terms. (e) Using a sense of humor to alleviate students' fear and embarrassment. W's lighthearted, entertaining manner harmonized with students' interests and the beat of repeated concepts. (f) Challenging students constantly to combine forms, such as human and animal shapes. (g) Ritualizing studio activities, such as plastering and painting techniques, by emphasizing the secrets of the trade. Gombrich (1984) advocates talk about how all artists repeat and borrow schema as "learned tricks if only from other pictures seen" (p. 50). (h) Developing a final student self-evaluation sheet that includes questions on what students specifically learned about culture and art history as well as studio. (i) Using the participant observation tools (questionnaires, worksheets, interviews, video and audio taping) to help learn more about students' diverse abilities and needs.

FUTURE IMPLICATIONS

Participant observation research can describe the realities of art teaching that make studies of teaching more believable. The views of the instructor, the students, outside observers, and the researcher fuse into an understandable account of teaching and learning. The vivid anecdotes may be so useful as to provide a script for those teachers who dread devising their own. Participant observation reveals what works, what doesn't, and what all participants suggest as improvements. Research tools then become teaching tools to share with other teachers, especially in video form. More such cooperative research on the everyday teaching at the middle school level is needed.

NOTES

1. A special thank you to Larry Woodson, participating art teacher from Fees Intermediate School in Tempe, Arizona, and graduate students Angela LaPorte and Lisa Wells. This research is sponsored by a grant from The Arizona Arts Education Research Institute.

2. Slow learners are those students who have learning disabilities related to slow maturation or a temporary developmental lag. They are often immature and poorly integrated, and need more time and help (Lerner, 1971/81, pp. 160-161). Add to this their cultural differences and lack of art experiences, and the reasons for learning difficulties are compounded.

3. PALS refers to Program for Alternative Learning, in which students with learning disabilities are assisted and mainstreamed in regular classes. W informed me that he didn't need to help the PALS students as much because their PALS teacher had attended the art class for three years and assisted her students.

4. When asked on a pre-questionnaire what art was, 15% of the students mentioned drawing and 12% mentioned feelings. When I asked what their favorite art project was, 27% responded drawing and 19% painting. They had few dislikes because of their limited art experiences. They initially found their teacher to be helpful, understanding, and "cool." Most responses are similar to responses of middle school students in the Midwest (Stokrocki, 1990).

5. The *Diablo* also is part of the Pascola clown mask tradition at the Yaqui Easter Enactment, somewhat similar to the Hopi and Zuni mud heads (Toor, 1985). In the Spring mask making unit, W discussed the Yaqui Easter celebration. He showed a video clip of the Yaqui deer dance. The performer wore the deer head on his cap and imitated the deer's graceful and cautious movements. The deer dancer symbolizes all "good animals" and is feared by the masked Fariseos, who represent "bad animals" and evil people who are against Jesus (From the Yaqui Lent and Easter Ceremonies 1992 flyer, Guadalupe, AZ). W invited his students to accompany him on Holy Saturday to the re-enactment in Guadalupe.

6. W complained that he often overextended himself and noted that during the last five weeks, he "logged-in" over 120 after-school hours with students.

7. W taught another unit on the art of Mesopotamia, a desert culture, and compared the gangs and battles of then with present-day examples. This lesson was videotaped and is the focus of another study.

8. Alexander (1983) reported how a high school art teacher used performance rituals, similar to a shaman, when teaching art history. Wilson (1977) also exlored the special "rites of passage" in her teaching of drawing to high school students.

REFERENCES

Addiss, S., & Erickson, M. (1993). *Art history and education.* Chicago: University of Illinois Press.

Alexander, R. (1977). Educational criticism of three art history classes (Doctoral dissertation, Stanford University, 1977). *Dissertation Abstracts International, 38,* 5195A, 78–2125.

Alexander, R. (1983). The art teacher as shaman: An educational criticism. *Studies in Art Education, 25* (1), 48–57.

Anglin, J. (1993). Three views of middle school art curriculum. *Studies in Art Education, 35* (1), 55–64.

Arizona Essential Skills. (1988). Phoenix, AZ: Arizona Department of Education.

Crizmac. (1988). *Tribal design* [videotape]. Tucson, AZ: Crizmac.

Day, M. (1969). The compatibility of art history and studio art activity in the junior high school art program: A comparison of two methods of teaching art history. *Studies in Art Education, 10* (2), 57–65.

Galbraith L., & Spomer, M. (1986). Does art history go to school? *Art Education, 39*(5), 10–13.

Gombrich, E. (1984). Truth and Stereotype. In P. Werhane, *Philosophical issues in art.* Englewood Cliffs, NJ: Prentice Hall.

LaPorte, A. (1993). [Personal participant observation records]. Unpublished raw data, Arizona State University, Tempe, AZ.

Lerner, J. (1981). *Learning disabilities: Theories, diagnosis, and teaching strategies* (3rd ed.). Boston: Houghton Mifflin.

Pomar, M. (1987). *El dia de los Muertes: The life of the dead in Mexican folk art.* (Available from Fort Worth Art Museum, Fort Worth, Texas).

Stokrocki, M. (1990). A cross-site analysis: Problems in teaching art to preadolescents. *Studies in Art Education, 31*(2), 106–117.

Toor, F. (1985). *A treasury of Mexican folkways.* New York: Bonanza.

Turner, V. (1969). *The ritual process.* Chicago: Aldine.

Wells, L. (1992). *An educational criticism of a junior high Art I class.* Unpublished undergraduate senior field work and project. Arizona State University, Tempe, AZ.

Wilson, M. (1977). Passage through communitas: An interpretive analysis of enculturation (Doctoral dissertation, Pennsylvania State University, 1977). *Dissertation Abstracts International, 38* (05), 2496-A.

Wilson, M. (1984). Theory into practice: The Whitehall story. In M. Day, E. Eisner, R. Stake, B. Wilson, & M. Wilson (Eds.), *Art history, art criticism, and art production* (pp. 1-28). Santa Monica, CA: Rand.

Zurmuehlen, M. (1983). Form and metaphor: A comparison of aesthetic structure in young children's pictures and stories. *Studies in Art Education, 24* (2), 118–117.

Sixth Grade Students' Development of Art Historical Understanding

Mary Erickson
Arizona State University

INTRODUCTION

Just how developmentally appropriate is art history instruction for middle school students? Can their aesthetic-understanding development be enhanced by art history instruction? Do middle school students have sufficiently developed inquiry strategies to prepare them to study art history? These are some of the issues which motivated me to study one class of sixth grade students over a period of one school year as they received art history instruction organized around ten roughly chronological, cross-cultural themes.[1]

Although a number of researchers have described young people's untutored responses to and preferences for artworks (Gardner & Gardner, 1971; Hardiman & Zernich, 1982; Neperud, Serlin, & Jenkins, 1986; Neperud & Stuhr, 1993; Taunton, 1980; Winston & Cupchik, 1992), less research has been done on the effects of instruction on students' understanding of artworks (Johnston, Roybol, & Parsons, 1988; Koroscik, Osman, & DeSouza, 1988; Koroscik, Short, & Stavropoulos, 1992; Silverman, Winner, Rosensteil, & Gardner, 1975). Writing about the development of aesthetic understanding, Parsons (1987) argues that "We reach later stages [of aesthetic understanding] only with an education in which we encounter works of art often and think about them seriously" (p. 27).

The sixth grade students I studied encountered approximately 100 artworks from various eras and cultures, organized around ten art historical themes. These students encountered the artworks often and thought about them seriously. Throughout the school year, the students listened to teacher presentations, took part in class discussions, and completed two worksheet packets on each of four artworks.

STUDENTS AND PROGRAM

The students in this study attended a suburban school serving lower-to-middle economic level households within a predominantly

The number of students with a learning disability in the classes was higher than the average in the school.

Euro-American community. The number of students with a learning disability in the classes was higher than the average in the school. The participating art teacher and I planned the entire year's art program around the following themes entitled "Art Before History," "Art of the First Cities," "Where We Fit in the World," "Art and Religion," "When Cultures Meet," "The Art of Powerful Families," "Art and Revolution," "Art and Technology," "Art and the Individual," and "Art and the Global Village" (Addiss & Erickson, 1993). Related studio activities accompanied instruction on each art historical theme.

Over a period of several weeks, each student studied one artwork using two packets of inquiry-oriented worksheets consisting of short-answer and multiple-choice questions. The first packet focused on reproduction, restoration, basic facts, and description. The second packet focused on placing the artwork in its artworld context, natural context, functional context, and cultural context. After all this inquiry, students wrote answers to the following art historical interpretation questions: (a) "Why do you think the artist made the artwork look the way it does?" (b) "Why do you think the viewer back then[2] wanted to look at the artwork?" (c) "What does the artwork tell you about what people generally thought or believed back then?" and (d) "How do you see this artwork differently from the people back then?" Each student studied four different artworks in this manner during the course of the school year.

On three occasions during the year, I interviewed six students individually. The art teacher and classroom teacher selected these six students according to their perception of the students' understanding of art history: two students perceived to be high in their art historical understanding; two, middle; and two, low. During the questioning sessions, students had before them the artworks they had studied with their worksheet packets and selected the specific work they wanted to discuss. I first asked each of the questions which the students had already responded to in writing in their packets (Questions 1–4 above). After each art historical interpretation question, I asked these follow-up questions: "How do you know?" (or, "How can you tell?"); "How sure are you?"; "What would you need to know to be more sure?" (or, "How could you find out?"), and "What question can you ask to help you better understand this artwork?" (or, "What would you like to know about this artwork?"). I analyzed the students' written and oral responses in an effort to determine their level of aesthetic understanding and to determine their range of art historical inquiry strategies.

STAGES OF AESTHETIC UNDERSTANDING

What can students' efforts at art historical interpretation tell us about their aesthetic development? Parsons (1987) has hypothesized that people develop their aesthetic understanding within five distinguishable stages. He characterizes each stage as "a cluster of ideas, and not properties of persons" (p. 11). He writes further that "People are not stages, nor are stages labels for people. Rather, people use stages, one or more of them, to understand paintings" (p. 11).

Parsons found that "most elementary school children use stage two ideas. Many, but fewer, adolescents use (at times) ideas from stage three" (p. 12). Parsons (1988) has argued for follow-up studies "to determine what the maximum, rather than actual, development of various groups might be [after educational intervention]" (p. 114). In my study, I found indications of a higher level of understanding when those students were engaged in an extensive art history program.

Stage One

Parsons (1987) identifies the primary characteristics of stage one as "an intuitive delight in most paintings, a strong attraction to color, and a freewheeling associative response to subject matter" (p. 21). A number of the sixth grade students in this study wrote that they liked the artworks even though no question asked for their preference. Several students wrote that they liked the colors in paintings by Matisse, Van Gogh, Gauguin, and Kandinsky. I found no clear evidence of freewheeling association among the students' responses. Although some students did use stage one aesthetic understanding in their art historical interpretations, stage one responses did not dominate their interpretations.

Stage Two

Parsons (1987) identifies the dominant idea of stage two as the subject or representation. He identifies beauty, realism, and skill as the grounds for stage two judgments. Students often referred to beauty when explaining why a viewer "back then" wanted to look at an artwork. Students described a wide range of diverse objects as "beautiful" (a Chinese carved jade disk, Mesa Verde ruins, a tiled Islamic dome, and an initial page from the *Book of Kells*). The word *pretty* was even more commonly used referring to very different works such as a Hiroshige woodcut, a Jackson Pollack painting, Boucher and Gainsborough portraits, a Kandinsky painting, a nineteenth-century carved tombstone, and even Stonehenge.

Several of the works described as "beautiful" or "pretty" are not representational (Mesa Verde ruins, Stonehenge, the Islamic dome, Pollack's and Kandinsky's paintings). Rather than pointing back to the stage one, intuitive delight in all works, these responses to non-representational artworks seem more to indicate a transition to a higher level of understanding. One student wrote that "back then" viewers of the Pollack painting "liked art—without subjects," and then wrote, "I like the colors." Even though this student's preference seems to use stage one understanding, his response to the art historical question is more characteristic of stage three understanding, awareness of various points of view. Even though the student may not have understood how or why anyone would like an artwork without sub-

In my study, I found indications of a higher level of understanding when those students were engaged in an extensive art history program.

ject matter, he did understand that there have been people with other points of view who did like art without subject matter.

Another student responding to Mesa Verde proposed that the viewer "back then" might have thought, "It was interesting to look at and pretty, maybe." When discussing how she might have seen Mesa Verde differently from the people "back then," she wrote, "They might have thought it was unpractical [sic], when I think that it's very practical and pretty." This understanding of a point of view other than one's own is also evident in the following statements about Stonehenge: "I think it's pretty. They thought it was a calendar" or from another student, "I just see rocks, not a calendar."

In addition to the stage two norm of beauty, the sixth grade students sometimes used the stage two norms of realism and skill. One student explained that a prehistoric painting looked the way it did because "they didn't know really how to draw. . . . It doesn't really look like an animal." Another student wrote of a Paleo-African rock painting that "it's kind of sloppy."

Parsons (1987) describes a typical stage two understanding as "transparent"; that is, the artwork is seen as a transparent frame through which something else is viewed (p. 38). I did not find instances of that sort of transparency, but I did find another kind of transparency which I have elsewhere labeled *transparent artistry*. Transparent artistry assumes that "the artist's role [is] limited to the direct recording of perception" (Erickson, 1994, p. 75). I found only one instance of this assumption among the sixth grade students' responses. Explaining why Van Gogh wanted *Starry Night* to look the way it does, one student wrote that "he saw like this."

Some sixth grade students in my study do seem to have been confused in several ways. When asked why the artist wanted his sculpture of the Buddha to look the way it does, one student responded that the "artist looked like that and sat like that," confusing the sculptor with the subject of the sculpture. Another student responded to the same question, this time about a Greek sculpture of an archer, "Maybe he did it for a woman that he loved or something to show that he's stronger." This student also seems to have confused the artwork with the artist. This response is perhaps also an example of the freewheeling association sometimes characteristic of stage one understanding. Later in the interview the same student, when asked why a viewer "back then" might want to look at the Greek sculpture, said "Maybe he'd like to buy it for his castle." And when asked what the sculpture told him about what people generally thought or believed "back then," this student responded that "they were

One student explained that a prehistoric painting looked the way it did because "they didn't know really how to draw. . . . It doesn't really look like an animal."

pretty strong and liked Hercules and Leonardo." This student confused information from various time periods. Another student writing about why a prehistoric viewer might want to look at an ivory carved staff wrote "because it will be worth a lot of money." These three students clearly had difficulty distinguishing between time periods as well as between the artwork, the artist, and the subject.

Many of the students' responses referred to artworks as "beautiful" or "pretty." A few responses seemed to use realism or skill as standards. In summary, many sixth grade students in this study used some stage two aesthetic understanding in their art historical interpretations.

Stage Three

Parsons (1987) identifies expressiveness as the dominant insight of stage three understanding. At this stage there is a new awareness of the artist and of the viewer. Parsons proposes that "there is skepticism about the value of talking about painting, and about the possibility of objective judgments, because the important criterion remains the quality of some individually felt experience" (p. 23).

The majority of students in the class were able to consider the artist's point of view as they responded to the question, "Why did the artist want the artwork to look the way it does?" Most were also able to speculate about the historical viewer's reactions to the painting when answering the question, "Why did the viewer back then want to look at the painting?" About a Greek sculpture of an archer, one student wrote, "He wanted to show how perfect people could be" and clearly proposed a motivation from the artist's point of view. Another student wrote about the historical viewers of David's *Oath of the Horatii* that "they wanted to be reminded of war and what it was like, and they liked old Greek stuff." The student clearly proposed a reaction from the perspective of a historical viewer.

Students were able to distinguish artist and viewer points of view; several were able to distinguish their own contemporary point of view from the point of view of someone of another time. When asked what a Chinese landscape told her about what people "back then" generally thought or believed, a student wrote "that man was small, nature big." When asked about how she saw the artwork differently from the people "back then," she wrote, "It reminds me of the stories my mother told me about Guam." She was able to distinguish her own association with the painting from responses reflective of the culture within which the painting was produced. Similarly, a student writing about an African mask wrote that "they wanted it to look

Many of the students' responses referred to artworks as "beautiful" or "pretty."

valuable, because the beads were expensive," and later, "We see it looking funny and weird." These responses also clearly evidenced the student's ability to distinguish his own point of view from that of another culture.

Some students in this study used stage two and even stage one aesthetic understanding. However, the majority of students were able to distinguish points of view, a skill indicative of stage three understanding.

Stage Four

Parsons (1987) identifies the new insight of stage four as the understanding "that the significance of a painting is a social rather than an individual achievement" (p. 24). During follow-up interviews most students displayed a rudimentary understanding of the value of a community of viewers as they explained how they might become more sure of their historical interpretations. They regularly referred to books, the library, movies, or classes as sources for further insight. Students' understanding that there are people (or books) whom they might consult for further information suggests that they may have moved beyond the stage three skepticism about the value of talking about art. Perhaps some sixth grade students are ready to be introduced to the community of viewers whose shared interpretations are characteristic of stage four aesthetic understanding.[3]

Stage Five

Parsons (1987) characterizes stage five understanding as based on the insight "that the individual must judge the concepts and values with which the tradition constructs the meaning of works of art" (p. 25). Not surprisingly, no sixth grade student in this study evidenced this level of understanding.

INQUIRY STRATEGIES

What can students' efforts at art historical interpretation tell us about their art historical inquiry strategies? How do students approach the task of understanding an artwork within the culture that produced it? My interviews with individual high-, middle-, and low-achieving sixth grade students offer some evidence of various strategies.

When asked follow-up questions such as "What would you need to know to be more sure?" or "How could you find out?", one student had no inquiry strategy and simply said, "I don't know." Other students were a little more clear about the problem and responded "Well, they were there back then when they made that [Mesa Verde], and I wasn't," and we need to "see them through the eyes of a different person." Another inventive student proposed jokingly, "I could

How do students approach the task of understanding an artwork within the culture that produced it?

use a time machine." Several students recalled information presented in class and applied it to the same or other artworks in their attempts at interpretation. For example, Confucius' ideas of social order and Taoist views about the importance of nature were applied to Chinese and Japanese artworks.

Seeking information from books was a commonly proposed strategy. Students mentioned that they might go to the library, or consult a dictionary or an encyclopedia. Other students were more focused in their search for information specifying art books, social studies books, or a movie on the artist. One student would "find out who made this one and see if he's written anything or read about him;" another wondered "if she [Judy Chicago] had anything like a philosophy written about this [*The Dinner Party*]." A third student said that she needed "to know how they thought and then maybe I could sort of think the way they did and figure out why they did it."[4]

Other more advanced strategies of art historical inquiry included references to details in the artworks being studied (e.g. subject matter details in sculptures and paintings and functional details in buildings) and comparisons with artworks made around the same time. When answering the question about why a Greek viewer "back then" might want to look at the archer sculpture, one student responded that "there are other artists' works like that, and if they are compared and proved that they have such delicate pieces, that would make me a little more sure that the Greek person wanted to look at them because there were so many around." One student expressed a concern of many of today's scholars when he said, concerning the meaning of a Chinese ritual bronze, "We can't be sure because we don't have ceremonies like this these days."[5]

If the students selected for the interviews were representative of their class, most of these sixth grade students had some strategy for art historical inquiry. A few of those strategies were rather sophisticated.

CONCLUSIONS

Let me conclude by returning to the three questions introducing this study. How developmentally appropriate is art history instruction for middle school students? If these sixth grade students are at all representative of middle school students in general, then there is evidence that art history instruction is quite appropriate. Despite the fact that a few students in this study seemed occasionally confused in several ways, most students were able to consider artworks from the perspectives of artist and viewer. Quite a few students were able to consider specific distinctions between their own responses and the responses of people of another time or culture.

Can middle school students' aesthetic understanding be enhanced by art historical instruction? Using Parsons' stages of aesthetic understanding as a guide, the sixth grade students in this study seem to

Other more advanced strategies of art historical inquiry included references to details in the artworks being studied.

> The results of this study suggest that serious, thoughtful art historical inquiry—oriented encounters may contribute to the development of students' aesthetic understanding.

have a more developed understanding than one might have imagined. Although stage two and even some stage one understandings were sometimes used, when challenged with specific art historical interpretation questions, most students were able to use stage three understanding in their responses. A number of students even showed some indication of a readiness for stage four insights. Parsons' stages are based on responses to eight Western (mostly modern) artworks discussed without any contextual information, and, as he articulates, "We reach later stages only with an education in which we encounter works of art often and think about them seriously" (1987, p. 27). The results of this study suggest that serious, thoughtful art historical inquiry-oriented encounters may contribute to the development of students' aesthetic understanding.

Do middle school students have sufficiently developed inquiry strategies to prepare them to study art history? The repertoire of inquiry strategies evidenced in the student interviews is quite broad, ranging from none to rather sophisticated. The use of inquiry-oriented worksheet packets and class discussion in which speculation was encouraged may have contributed to the range of strategies exhibited by students in their interviews. Even if we assume that sophisticated art historical inquiry strategies are undeveloped in most middle school students, this does not compel us to leave students without such strategies. Presumably, systematic inquiry-oriented instruction can develop a range of inquiry strategies beyond the base which sixth grade students exhibit prior to instruction. The anecdotal evidence resulting from this study does support such a presumption.

Convincing middle school art teachers that their students are capable of art historical understanding is just one of many tasks which must be addressed before one can hope that art history instruction will become commonplace in middle school art curricula. Anglin (1993) has recently documented the small percentage of middle school art appreciation instruction in the Midwest. She writes that there is "little consistent attention . . . given to formal art appreciation, art history, or criticism activities in the observed classrooms" (p. 60). In interviews she discovered that teachers "emphasized media and production activities" [because] they "found art production to be satisfying and a successful way of including art in the lives of middle school students." Teachers "wrote and taught curriculum based on their own successful experiences rather than on theoretical models of outcome or content" (p. 61). She suggests that themes of interest to adolescents might be used to help "broaden [students'] understanding and make production more meaningful" (p. 63). This study of sixth grade students' developing art historical understanding provides evidence of the successful experience of one art teacher (and cooperating researcher) in including art history as a major component of a middle school art curriculum. Perhaps the breadth of the ten art historical themes also contributed to the students' interest.

Stokrocki (1993a, 1993b) also has documented several middle school art teachers' successful experiences in teaching art history.

More research and in-school successes may be required to convince art teachers to increase art historical content in their middle school curricula. Perhaps the art historical understanding of the sixth grade students documented in this study will encourage art teachers and researchers to continue to plan and document successful art history experiences upon which the field can be built with confidence.

NOTES

1. This study is part of a larger study funded by the Arizona Arts Education Research Institute, co-authored with Susan Raymond, who was also the participating art teacher in the study.
2. A few of the 100 artworks used in this study in association with the last theme, Art and the Global Village, were made as little as thirteen years prior to the study. Thirteen years in the lives of sixth grade students is very much "back then." However, as an era for historical, or art historical reflection, it is quite recent. One might question whether sixth grade students can be expected to have adequate prior knowledge to be able to distinguish differences between making and responding to art today and making and responding to art as little as thirteen years ago.
3. DiBlasio (1988) has proposed that Parsons "extend his observations to students whose understanding of art is being formed . . . by substantive art programs, so that their experience also can be reflected in the conception of developmental stages" (p. 107).
4. This strategy is remarkably similar to the method of "historical imagination" described by Collingwood in *The Idea of History* (1946): "To know someone else's activity of thinking is possible only on the assumption that this same activity can be re-enacted in one's own mind. In that sense, to 'know what someone is thinking' (or 'has thought') involves thinking it for one's self" (p. 289).
5. Saville (1982) enters the contemporary debate on our freedom to imagine the experience of people of the past. He states that even though "this freedom is not limitless and that sometimes we cannot revive the art of the past does not argue for despising the labour of trying to acquire often inaccessible and recondite information in the light of which a given work may need to be understood. It says merely that we may have to undertake that labour to understand the art of the past . . . . "(p. 52). In response to Saville, Richmond (1992) writing specifically about teaching art historical interpretation argues, "the capacity to overstep, to some extent, inadequacies of evidence and temporal and cultural distances by imaginatively reconstructing past meanings [should] be called . . . plausible rather than . . . irrefutable . . . ." (p. 39).

More research and in-school successes may be required to convince art teachers to increase art historical content in their middle school curricula.

REFERENCES

Addiss, S., & Erickson, M. (1993). *Art history and education*. Urbana and Chicago: University of Illinois Press.

Anglin, J. M. (1993). Three views of middle school art curriculum. *Studies in Art Education, 35*(1), 55–64.

Collingwood, R. G. (1946). *The idea of history*. London: Oxford University Press.

DiBlasio, M. (1988). Educational application of *How We Understand Art:* An analysis. *Journal of Aesthetic Education, 22*(4), 103–107.

Erickson, M. (1994). Evidence for art historical interpretation referred to by young people and adults. *Studies in Art Education, 35*(2), 71–78.

Gardner, H., & Gardner, J. (1971). Developmental trends in sensitivity to painting style and subject matter. *Studies in Art Education, 12*(1), 11–16.

Hardiman, G. W., & Zernich, T. (1982). The relative influence of parts and wholes in shaping preference responses to paintings. *Studies in Art Education, 23*(2), 31–38.

Johnston, M., Roybol C., & Parsons, M. J. (1988). Teaching the concept of style to elementary school age students: A developmental investigation. *Visual Arts Research, 14*(2), 57–67.

Koroscik, J. S., Osman, A. H., & DeSouza, I. (1988). The function of verbal mediation in comprehending works of art: A comparison of three cultures. *Studies in Art Education, 29*(2), 91–102.

Koroscik, J. S., Short, G., & Stavropoulos, C. (1992). Frameworks for understanding: The function of comparative art contexts and verbal clues. *Studies in Art Education, 33*(3), 154–164.

Neperud, R. W., Serlin, R., & Jenkins, H. (1986). Ethnic aesthetics: The meaning of ethnic art for Blacks and non-Blacks. *Studies in Art Education, 28*(1), 16–29.

Neperud, R. W., & Stuhr, P. L. (1993). Cross-cultural valuing of Wisconsin Indian art by Indians and non-Indians. *Studies in Art Education, 34*(4), 244–253.

Parsons, M.J. (1987). *How we understand art: A cognitive developmental account of aesthetic experience*. New York: Cambridge University Press.

Parsons, M. J. (1988). Assumptions about art and artworld: A response to critics. *Journal of Aesthetic Education, 22*(4), 107–116.

Richmond, S. (1992). Historicism, teaching, and the understanding of works of art. *Visual Arts Research, 18*(1), 32–41.

Saville, A. (1982). *The test of time: An essay in philosophical aesthetics*. New York: Oxford University Press.

Silverman, J., Winner, E., Rosensteil, A. K., & Gardner, H. (1975). On training sensitivity to painting styles. *Perception, 4*, 373–384.

Stokrocki, M. (1993a). A microethnographic study of a middle school art teacher: Instructing low achievers through electronic media. Manuscript submitted for publication.

Stokrocki, M. (1993b). A microethnographic study of how a middle school art teacher integrates art history with art making. Manuscript submitted for publication.

Taunton, M. (1980). The influence of age on preference for subject matter, realism, and spatial depth in painting reproductions. *Studies in Art Education, 21*(3), 40–52.

Winston, A. S., & Cupchik, G. C. (1992). The evaluation of high art and popular art by naive and experienced viewers. *Visual Arts Research, 18*(1), 1–14.

Socially Relevant Art Criticism: A Semiotic Approach to Art Criticism in Art Education

Gaye Leigh Green
University of Georgia

Central to the teaching of art education is the interpretation of works of art. Through the study of visual images, students encounter meaning about the world and their relationships with it. While historically much time and thought has been devoted to teaching children how to make art, much less consideration has been given to the ways in which art criticism can be taught. Currently, most art educators use a four step methodology that follows a sequential process of description, analysis, interpretation, and evaluation (Feldman, 1970). While this methodology provides students an opportunity to discover information about the work, it does not necessarily facilitate the rich and meaningful understanding that can emerge when this format is presented in conjunction with other instructional approaches.

A number of art educators of the 90s have been persistent in their efforts to promote an approach to art criticism that considers the study of the work of art and its context, the artist, and the perceiver. Kristin Congdon (1989) observes that "current art criticism formats represent a structure that gives tremendous insight into the Anglo academic way of seeing and understanding art, yet exclude to some degree knowledge about other cultural groups and their art forms" (p. 177). Elizabeth Garber (1990) notes that it is important to integrate "gender, race, class and ethnic considerations into the curricula" (p. 17), while Wasson, Stuhr, and Petrovich-Mwaniki (1990) suggest "a socio-anthropological basis for studying the aesthetic production and experience of cultures, which means focusing on knowledge about the makers of art, as well as the sociological context in which the work is produced" (p. 235). Contemporary thought in art education proposes that there is more to studying the work of art than can be ascertained by a method of art criticism that focuses primarily on the work of art to the exclusion of studying the role that the artist, the context, and the perceiver play in the interpretive process.

Figure 1. Leonora Carrington. *Self Portrait.* 1936–37. oil/canvas. 54.77 x 88.9 cm (25.5 x 32"). Private collection. Photograph: Courtesy of Pierre Matisse Foundation, NY.

The implementation of a semiotic perspective in the process of art criticism can make teaching more "relevant and meaningful" (Garber, 1990, p. 17). Semiotician Umberto Eco (1989) has delineated three areas: authorship, reception, and context as being crucial to the critical process stating that the core of semiotic theory lies "within the dialectus between the sender, the addressee and the context," (p. 45). In an application to art education, it would be important to emphasize the relationship between the artist, the perceiver, and the context of the work of art.

Although this strategy can enrich the interpretation of works of art from all cultures, Leonora Carrington's *Self-Portrait* (1936–37) will be used to illustrate the various components of a semiotic strategy (see Figure 1). Rich in visual imagery, the painting features a woman who is motioning to a seemingly menacing creature which most viewers interpret as a lactating hyena. A tailless rocking horse hovers on the wall behind the woman and mysteriously floats above her head. Through the window, we see a white horse frolicking in the green outdoors in distinct contrast to the serious, somewhat somber, otherworldly atmosphere of the interior scene.

Carrington is a British Surrealist who, while in her early twenties, was introduced to the tenets of Surrealism by Max Ernst. Her body of work includes paintings, drawings, etchings, sculpture, and an equally impressive array of literary works which make Carrington not only an edifying artist for students to study but also one who is equally fascinating and compelling for further research.

AUTHORSHIP

The first area identified by Eco (1989) as crucial to the study of works of art is that of authorship, the study of artists who create works of art. A mode of scholarship that has been employed for hundreds of years by art historians from Vasari to present-day feminist critics such as Lucy Lippard, the study of an artist informs the viewer, humanizes the interpretive process, and encourages an enduring impression that will often outlast the specifics of a less comprehensive interpretation.

To help students discover important information about the life of an artist, research can be completed by either the teacher or the students and should consider ten different contexts: (1) historical, (2) political, (3) religious, (4) philosophical, (5) economic, (6) artistic, (7) cultural, (8) geographic, (9) psychological, and (10) scientific. Each of these contexts involves the discoveries, inquiry, and scholarship that has been completed in each area of endeavor. Students can be given a chart outlining the ten contexts, and the content of each can be discussed. For example, if students or teachers choose to explore a political context as being relevant to the work of art, they might consider the political system in which the artist worked, the ramifications of politics on the artist's work, or the prevalent political theories which

If the cultural context is selected for study, students and teachers might consider exploring the literature of the time period in which the work was created, to discover any relationships between the creation of written works and visual images.

Study of the context in which a work of art was created can provide a vast array of information and demonstrates the ongoing process that meaningful interpretive strategies embrace.

operated within the time and locale of the artist. An example of the influence of political occurrences in Carrington's life was her mental breakdown that resulted from the Nazi regime's incarcerations of Max Ernst, with whom she had maintained a close personal relationship.

If the cultural context is selected for study, students and teachers might consider exploring the literature of the time period in which the work was created, to discover any relationships between the creation of written works and visual images. Again, Carrington's life provides a cogent example of this influence. An inordinate number of literary works inform her imagery from Cocteau's *Les Enfantes Terribles* that she read as a teenager, to her adult interest in the writings of mystic Gurdieff and Celtic author Robert Graves. Looking at the specifics of the life and work of an artist can provide important clues which enrich the student's understanding of works of art.

RECEPTION

Reception, the process of perceiving works of art, is also identified by Eco (1989) as an essential component of the critical process. To understand the impact of what students bring to the work of art in terms of background and experience, I ask them to reflect on a series of questions that intentionally begin on a general level and proceed to one that is more personal. Examples of questions that I ask students to consider are:

> How do you think the location of your birth affects the ways in which you view the world? Consider the town, state, and country in which you were born. What about the time period? Consider the music, movies, books, and television programs that are popular within your culture. How do they affect the way that you live and think? Consider the president or other important leaders of your country. Do they affect the ways that you look at the world? Can you think of anything about yourself personally that affects your perception, such as your relationships with friends, your religion, the way that you were raised, your place within your family, how you succeed in school, your personality, or experiences that you have had such as traveling or relationships with friends?

When a group of pre-service elementary education students were asked to think about how they perceived Carrington's self-portrait, individual comments about gender and how it influences perception led one student to share that she is "a strong believer in the equality of women." She continued, noting that she lives "in a small rural town where girls get pregnant. They do not have much education and are dependent on their husbands or boyfriends. These women are so dependent on their husbands or boyfriends that they do not have the opportunity to be aggressive, strong, or well-educated."

On the other hand, after a male student discussed his traditional upbringing wherein the women in his "family were housewives and did not hold down full-time paying jobs," and that in this work of art "once again a woman wanted power," this student quoted his grandfather who once told him that "a woman is never happy unless she has it all!" The two students' opposing views regarding gender roles reveal the individual perspectives that they use to view works of art.

CONTEXT

The third area that Eco outlines as crucial to the interpretive process is context, or the situation, background, or environment from which the work emerges. In order to better understand the context in which the work of art was created, I ask students to consider the following questions:

> How might working in a particular century affect the ways that works of art are created? Would living in a specific country, such as the United States, affect the way an artist thinks and works and, if so, how? Are there elements in the work of art that symbolize something? If so, does the symbol mean the same thing now that it did in the time in which the work was created? Does it mean something unique to your generation? Can you think of any reference books that might help you understand the symbols or elements of the work of art? When and where was the work made? For what purpose and for whom was it made? What do you think it meant?

Concerning Carrington's self-portrait, learning about the historical developments in early twentieth century Europe would help students understand the significant repercussions in Carrington's life and work that resulted from Hitler's invasion of Europe. Study of the context in which a work of art was created can provide a vast array of information and demonstrates the ongoing process that meaningful interpretive strategies embrace.

IMPLICATIONS FOR ART CRITICISM IN ART EDUCATION

A semiotic approach to art criticism suggests an expansive and ongoing dialogue between viewers and works of art that transcends a step-by-step approach. Semiotics calls for continual dialogue between an audience and a work of art. Interpretive strategies of this nature are evolutionary. They differ according to the characteristics of the audience and the time period within which that audience perceives

Semiotics calls for continual dialogue between an audience and a work of art.

the work. Interpretations developed within this mindset present an exploratory search for meaning rather than an adherence to a particular method that remains constant for each interpretation.

Implementing a semiotic approach to art criticism is especially relevant at the middle school level as students are becoming capable of the research skills needed to study works from a semiotic perspective and have reached a position in their schooling when study of nationally related issues are central to the curriculum. Research into the life of the artist and the various contexts that surround the work of art can be completed and presented by the teacher, assigned to students for personal research, or undertaken as a collaborative project whereby student and teacher work together to gather information and produce an insightful interpretation and understanding of the work. Thus, research of this nature requires the individual adaptation of teachers according to their specific curricular needs.

Using the foundation of semiotics not only enriches the interpretive process by teaching the students about other cultures, the nature of perception, the lives of artists, and the creative act, but it also enhances students' knowledge of themselves and their relationships to the world. And what better goal could be set for art education instruction than the wonders of self-discovery!

REFERENCES

Congdon, K. (1989). Multicultural approaches to art criticism. *Studies in Art Education, 30*(3), 176–184.

Eco, U. (1989). *The open work.* Boston: Harvard University Press.

Feldman, E. B. (1970). *Becoming human through art.* Englewood Cliffs, NJ: Prentice-Hall.

Garber, E. (1990). Implications of feminist art criticism for art education. *Studies in Art Education, 32*(1), 17–26.

Wasson, R., Stuhr, R., & Petrovich-Mwaniki, L. (1990). Teaching art in the multicultural classroom: Six position statements. *Studies in Art Education, 31*(4), 234–246.

Combining Poetry and Visual Art in a Museum Setting: An Interdisciplinary Program for Sixth Graders

INTRODUCTION

Marilyn Wolf-Ragatz
*Clarke County
School District
Athens, Georgia*

Art educators agree that students need to view original works of art and that art museums offer that opportunity (Henry, 1992). By responding to works of art, students are able to participate in active learning, analyzing, and reflection. They are able to concentrate on the art objects and discover new concepts. As Walsh-Piper (1994) states, ". . . the experience of a museum visit, from the aesthetics of the architectural setting to the personal encounter with a great work of art, is one with the potential for wonder and awe, creating memorable images for the child" (p. 1). In a typical museum lesson at The Getty Museum, for example, students may write poetry, debate philosophies, or hypothesize original purposes of historic objects (Brigham and Robinson, 1992). Diane Brigham of the Getty states, "Whether we are looking at details to help us piece together a story from long ago, or writing poems to express a painting's mood, young people are always enticed to think about what they have seen" (Walsh-Piper, 1994, p. 1). It has also been shown that students recall much more about the paintings they viewed if there were verbalization and visual association (Franke, Levin, and Carney, 1991).

This chapter describes "Poets in the Gallery," a program that provided a group of sixth-grade students the opportunity to visit the Georgia Museum of Art to experience an exhibition of paintings, write poetry describing those paintings, and create illustrations for the poems. Each stage of the program is explained and can serve as a guide for others interested in providing meaningful museum experiences for middle school students. The benefits to students, teachers, and museum personnel are elaborated upon, and observations about the program's effectiveness are included.

Our adventure in poetry writing and illustration began when, with the support of my middle school principal, I developed a discipline-based art education curriculum for sixth-grade students. The curriculum was designed to integrate art with the core subjects and was called *Creative Expression*. For the first time, art was moved from a separate building which housed the arts and physical education classes to the academic area of the school. As was true of math, science, English, literature, and social studies, *Creative Expression* was scheduled each day of the school year for all sixth grade students, allowing me the opportunity to interact daily with the academic teachers and to coordinate the design of my curriculum with theirs.

Prior to the beginning of the new school year, I shared my goals with Susan Longhenry, then the Curator of Education at the Georgia Museum of Art in Athens, Georgia. Longhenry was interested in developing a stronger relationship between the museum and the district schools; we both wanted to introduce the students to a museum experience that would allow them to become more comfortable with the museum's resources. Longhenry was particularly interested in designing a program similar to one that originated at the Chicago Art Institute which introduced students to a professional poet in the museum setting and culminated in the students' writing poetry about selected paintings. We agreed that the concept was good but that the program could be expanded through our consulting and working with the sixth-grade English and literature teachers. We decided to invite a professional children's poet to work with the students and teachers and to have the students illustrate their poetry.

PROGRAM PLANNING

We began the planning process by sharing our objectives with the English and literature teachers whose students would participate. They were receptive and enthusiastic about the program in part because poetry is an important component of the sixth-grade language arts curriculum in Georgia, and they thought that this approach would be a creative way to introduce the subject. English, literature, and visual arts would be combined in an interdisciplinary program in which students could learn to improve communication skills through the arts. The teachers were also supportive of the fact that every student, including the special education students, would have the opportunity to participate.

With agreement for our goals firmly established, we began the search for a recognized, well-published children's poet who would be accessible to our students. One of the literature teachers suggested the perfect candidate, Athens' resident Mary Ann Coleman, a nationally recognized children's poet who recently published her fifth book, and quickly secured a promise from her to hear our proposal. After we discussed our ideas, Coleman enthusiastically accepted the invitation to work with our students for a two-week period the following spring. Coleman attended our planning meetings and assisted us in coordinating the details of our project's curriculum.

Subsequent to Coleman's acceptance of the plan, we submitted a state Artist-in-Residence grant proposal to the Georgia Council for the Arts. This grant is designed to financially compensate artists who spend a significant period of time working in public schools. As a requirement of the application, a business sponsor must match any grant funds that are awarded. Three local businesses agreed to match the grant by funding a publication of the students' poetry and illustrations. The Georgia Museum of Art offered to host a formal reception for the students and Coleman at the conclusion of the program. We began feeling confident that our plans would be successful when we received approval for the grant a few weeks later.

The "Poets in the Gallery" program was scheduled for the first two weeks of March. One of the most crucial considerations in planning this program was to schedule the activity during a time when the museum was exhibiting works of art with appropriate and relative subject matter for sixth-grade students. We planned our program to coincide with an exhibition of paintings by Andree Ruellan. Again, destiny worked in our favor. Ruellan, a spry, 93-year-old charmer, trained in Paris and now living in up-state New York, was the perfect choice for the program. As described in the exhibition catalog, "Ruellan represents America through images that are strongly affected by her warm, compassionate perception of people" (Keyes, 1993, p.1). Although she painted subjects representing various areas of the country, the majority of her work focused on the South. The fact that "she depicted a segment of the population normally overlooked by mainstream artists, namely, African-Americans" (Keyes, p.2) was especially relevant to our school's culturally diverse population and made the choice of her exhibit even more appropriate.

In January, we began preparing the students for the program. Art criticism skills are a central part of my curriculum because I believe that they are crucial to the development of visual literacy. We had practiced these skills throughout the year, and, when this project began, I reemphasized their value. Using Feldman's (1984) method of art criticism as a guide, the sixth-graders became quite adept at description, analysis, interpretation, and evaluation. The English and literature teachers also began introducing students to various forms of poetry and familiarizing them with the work of respected poets as well as the less familiar works of their peers.

The Ruellan exhibition opened three weeks prior to our "Poets in the Gallery" program. Although there had been an unusually large snowfall in New York, Ruellan chose to battle the weather and attend the opening reception at the Georgia Museum of Art. She reacted with enthusiasm when told that her paintings would serve as the motivation for the children's writing and drawing. She was especially pleased when informed that the students would be spending considerable time during the program at the museum. Typical of what we found to be her generous nature, she explained that she would not be staying in town but would be happy to answer any questions the students might have about both her life and her paintings. The following

With agreement for our goals firmly established, we began the search for a recognized, well—published children's poet who would be accessible to our students.

day, the children developed ten questions and mailed them to Ruellan. Only days later, an audiotape of her responses arrived. She was informative, honest, funny, and caring as she answered each question. The reaction from the students was surprisingly positive. They listened intently to her explanations and, after hearing the tape, thought of many more questions they would like to ask her. They then understood that they were about to work with two professional artists: poet, Mary Ann Coleman, and visual artist, Andree Ruellan.

One week prior to Coleman's scheduled classroom visit, Longhenry visited each class to introduce the students to the historical background and to provide an overview of Ruellan's work. She showed many slides of Ruellan's paintings and discussed them with the students, placing greater emphasis on Ruellan's background and motivation and less emphasis on criticism. We wanted the students to have as broad an exposure to Ruellan's work as possible prior to the museum visit.

Coleman officially came to the school the first week of March. However, she met with the English and literature teachers and discussed her methods of teaching poetry, reviewed information to be introduced to the students, planned what she would teach, and familiarized herself with the school's procedures much earlier. She was introduced to the sixth graders at two assembly programs and spent the following four days in the classroom of each English and literature teacher, working one-on-one with the students.

Coleman's teaching skills held the students' attention throughout each class period; each child worked intensely to complete the assignments. As she guided the children through the development of their poetry-writing skills, she often stopped to read some successful examples of other children's works, motivating the students to continue their efforts. During her time in the classrooms, she had each student select an art reproduction from her postcard collection. They were asked to follow the stages of art criticism in viewing the painting pictured on the card and then write a poem about it as practice in preparation for the upcoming museum experience.

The Georgia Museum of Art is fairly small, necessitating a limit on the number of students who can visit at one time. Consequently, we scheduled five field trips of fifty students each. The students were brought into the galleries where Reullan's paintings were on exhibit. A docent directed the students to the gallery that held approximately 50 of Ruellan's paintings and explained the changes in subject matter and painting style throughout Ruellan's career. The students were then asked to select a favorite painting. During a two-hour period, each child was to critique his or her selected painting and write a poem about that work. Students moved slowly through the galleries, drawn to some paintings, passing others. It took several minutes for most to select the work they liked best. For others, it seemed an impossible task. Our rule was that a maximum of three students could select the same painting to avoid crowding and repetition of subject matter. I noticed that there were clearly a few favorite paintings: *Pink*

The children lay on the floor, sat with legs crossed, or sat back-to-back as they began carefully making notes and critiquing selected works of art.

Masks, Louisiana Landscape, and *Marketplace.* A few sixth graders made their selection based on the choice of a best friend. We observed that most students seemed very comfortable in the museum, perhaps because our school system encourages teachers to bring classes to the museum whenever possible, or perhaps it was because students were given more time than they would be allowed on a typical museum field trip. They were invited to become involved with the art and to be comfortable in the process. The children laid on the floor, sat with legs crossed, or sat back-to-back as they began carefully making notes and critiquing selected works of art. There was quiet conversation throughout the two-hour period, but students were intent on completing their finest poem. Out of 250 students, I found only two or three unable to begin writing and only one who could not decide which painting to select. Classroom exercises in art criticism and clear direction from Coleman in the writing of poetry made this possible.

Coleman, the teachers, and I attended each session at the museum. We wandered through the galleries making ourselves available to the students. However, much of the time students went directly to Coleman as they had quickly developed a respect for her as a professional poet, teacher, and friend. We were fascinated by the intelligent questions asked and perceptive comments made by the children. The students saw objects in the paintings we had never seen and sensed emotions we had not perceived until they brought them to our attention.

During the following week, the students reviewed their poems and made necessary adjustments. The teachers collected and reviewed the work for spelling and grammatical errors, and Coleman took a final look at the work. The teachers typed all 250 poems in preparation for the book layout. After the poems were typed, I introduced the technique of scratchboard illustration to the students. Rather than having the students illustrate their own poems, I distributed another student's poem to each child, being sure no child would both illustrate and write a poem about the same painting. We did this because we believed that if a student studied and wrote about a Ruellan painting he or she would be likely to complete an illustration that would too closely resemble the painting. If, however, the student illustrated a poem that described an unfamiliar painting, the student would be more likely to create a work of art that had a more personal style and interpretation.

The scratchboard technique was selected because the white lines of the drawings on a black background would contrast nicely to the black lines of the written poetry on white paper in the student book. In addition, Georgia's art curriculum for grade six requires the study of positive space and negative space, as well as of texture. The illustrations were completed by late April, and the process of designing a book layout and having it printed began. Each child and every painting was represented by a poem in the book. Although every child did

The scratchboard technique was selected because the white lines of the drawings on a black background would contrast nicely to the black lines of the written poetry on white paper in the student book.

complete an illustration, there was not enough room in the book to include all of them.

The grand finale to the program was an elegant reception at the museum. Lace cloths draped the tables. There were lavish flower arrangements and ornate silver trays of cookies and sweets. Music played in the background, and excited, well-dressed children entered with proud parents and relatives. The ceremony began with the introduction of Mary Ann Coleman. She praised the students and read several of her poems to the audience. Following her reading, approximately 25 students stepped up to the podium, one at a time, and read their poems. Speeches were made, and the finished book was unveiled (see Figure 1).

BENEFITS OF THE PROGRAM

There were many benefits from "Poets in the Gallery," the greatest being that every sixth-grade student participated. Every child worked on a personal level with Coleman. Each child had a poem published and completed an illustration. The quality of the student work was exceptional; this may, in part, be due to the students' working with professionals.

Figure 1. One of the participants enjoys sharing her work with a family member.

They were excited to work side-by-side with a recognized poet and amazed that a writer who was good enough to have poetry published would work with them. They were equally impressed that an artist whose paintings hung in a museum would take the time to answer their questions. The program's structure also contributed to its success. Assemblies, classroom visitors, and field trips all underscored the importance of the program. Finally, the knowledge that their work would be included in a book probably helped motivate the students to do well.

Another factor that lead to the program's success was the inclusion of special education students. Many of these children with special needs were normally separated from their peers for specific instructional help. We made no attempt to identify or separate children into learning categories. As a result, many of their poems and illustrations were equal to, if not better than, those of the other students.

Emphasis on art criticism skills helped students develop greater understanding of the paintings; thus, they were able to write more descriptive and expressive poetry. With such clearly described scenes and emotions, students were able to create detailed, illustrative scratchboard drawings.

The results of the "Poets in the Gallery" program supports the theory that integrated and interdisciplinary learning is beneficial to student success. The children developed a greater understanding of the arts and their value as a means for communication and personal expression. They learned that visual art goes well beyond the confines of the art classroom.

The children became more comfortable in the museum as the program progressed. Their "museum stiffness" vanished. They continued to respect the museum's rules, but they also moved freely through the galleries, discussing works that were interesting to them and conversing with the guards. One of the guards later told me that he thought it was the best program he had witnessed. He thought it was wonderful seeing the students enjoying themselves so much, and he particularly loved sharing information and conversation with them. We felt that our goal to enable students to develop a greater understanding of the museum's resources had been realized.

It is often difficult to involve parents in school activities at the middle school level due, in part, to the adolescent's desire to be as independent as possible. However, information was consistently sent home to explain the program and its progress. The parents later were able to celebrate their children's success at the museum reception giving them a chance to see first hand the depth of their children's involvement in the program.

OBSERVATIONS AND COMMENTS

It is important to middle school students to have finished products of which they can be proud. The book of poetry and illustrations was an especially appropriate product enabling each child, as well as friends and relatives, to have a copy. The finished book included comments from Coleman, Ruellan, Longhenry, the principal, and the teachers; it was documentation of the collaborative effort of each participant.

The local newspaper publicized the project by printing a full-page article with color photos and including examples of the children's poetry and illustrations. In the midst of all the negative news and political turmoil associated with public education, it was pleasant reading about an educational success. The resulting response from parents, citizens, and community leaders confirmed the importance of the program.

It is important to middle school students to have finished products of which they can be proud.

The school's principal made this final comment about the program:

> The "Poets in the Gallery" project this Spring could be used to illustrate the characteristics of middle schools that make them unique. The project centered around an Artist-in-Residence, distinguished author and poet, Mary Ann Coleman. It involved collaboration between the sixth-grade teachers working across different disciplines with one large group of learners. It involved some parental and volunteer assistance and visits to the community's Georgia Museum of Art creating a special link between the school and the community. It required personal expression and creativity as students studied works of art and responded to them in poetic and visual forms. (Mathis in *Poets in the Gallery*, 1992, Burney-Harris-Lyons Middle School Sixth Graders.)

Coleman reflected upon the successes of the students:

> I have always known that the young have an incredible ability to create uncommon things. They can do this because, unlike many adults, they can still see the world afresh, unhampered by ordinary, world-worn ways of seeing. Wordsworth was correct in saying that the child comes

Figure 2. The involvement of poet Mary Ann Coleman and visual artist Andree Ruellan made this museum experience especially meaningful to the students.

to the earth "trailing clouds of glory," a glory that is still present in all of us, but particularly in young people, as long as they continue to have the courage to express themselves in their own unique way.

These poems were selected from a variety of children representing slow, average, and gifted learners. It became evident that teaching through personal response to original works of art brought out the best in every child.

Pink Masks

Quietly, pink masks are still
with no face behind them.
Day goes on, night appears,
the masks are still
Dead flowers along a white, musty cloth,
petals falling one by one,
The moon shines as brightly as fire.
Shadows on the wall
move closer and closer to the masks.
The flowers become alive again,
but the masks fade away with the shadows.

by Desiree Tarquinio
from the painting, *Pink Masks*

Marketplace

African-Americans having
the time of their lives.
The sun glazes them,
making their faces
alluring. The children
barefoot and the sun
is burning their feet.
The men's sweat
rushing down their
faces making them
stronger as they
carry the fish and
shrimp to market.
The women, nurturing
voices louder and
louder, trying to sell
their food.

by Rene Wise
from the painting, *Marketplace*

A Dreary Day

A dreary day in the park
Women walking, their heads hung low,
Their umbrellas, dots of color.
The children slumping to and fro.
An occasional wagon creaks
On the cobblestone street.
The dark trees' shapes
Jut out and form shadows on
The gray sky.
The houses just blend together,
The street lamps, dim.
A young man sitting in the gazebo,
Lazy.
It has just rained,
The water still drips from
The iron gates.
The grass a dull green, the branches all wet
A dreary day in the park.

by Serena Fuller
from the painting, *April, Washington Square.*

The Beach

People lying along the beach,
grateful for the tide to touch fiery feet.
People swimming,
their bodies tasting the salt
from the blinding blue ocean.
The ocean. . . .
an alluring mirror.
Towels are deserted.
Tides crash in,
smearing sand like butter.
People go to their cars
leave the noise behind.
The beach is abandoned.

by Robbie Service
from the painting, *Beach at Whimple's Dam.*

The Kite Goes Away

A boy
flying a kite in
Spring winds, raises it
higher and higher. The children
want to play, too, but they must sit
upon the wall, struggle to get a
better view. Wind-filled, the
clothes hang out to dry;
children strain to
glimpse at the
tiny kite
as it
soars
from
view.
Higher,
   higher.
     String
       runs
    out;
children go home;
the
  wind
    dies
      down.

by Cassie Holt
from the painting, *Louisiana Landscape.*

A New Orleans Night

On a bridge in New Orleans,
I stand and feel the breeze,
as soft as a kitten's purr.
I see a glimmering street
shining its vibrant lights.
Blue moonlight shimmers
on the dark, cool waters.
Night and the trees sway
back and forth like an
unlocked gate as the sun
sets into the mist of the sky
to travel to the other
side of the world.

by John Tuggle
from the painting, *From Quai Montebello.*

The Accordionist

The blind man plays the accordion smoothly,
His accordion rattles as an empty
subway car goes by. Pigeons whimper
as they nervously search for food.
The man's life is as empty as his bag,
his days as rough as the subway grate
he sleeps on. He plays on a path
not welcome by strangers.
He only knows one tune but he knows it well.
The coldness of his hands bring a strange
texture to his music. The wind
rattles in and out of his tattered instrument.

by Brie Ellis
from the painting, *The Accordionist.*

REFERENCES

Brigham, D. & Robinson, J. (1992). From the guest editors. *Journal of Museum Education, 17*(2) 3.

Burney-Harris Lyons Middle School Sixth Graders. (1992). *Poets in the gallery.* (Available from Burney-Harris Lyons Middle School, Athens, GA).

Feldman, E. B. (1984). *Varieties of visual experience.* Englewood Cliffs, NJ: Prentice-Hall.

Franke, T., Levin, J., & Carney, R. (1991). Mnemonic artwork learning strategies: Helping students remember more than, "Who painted the what?" *Contemporary Educational Psychology, 16*, 375–390.

Henry, C. (1992). Retention and recall of images: Evaluating museum experiences of schoolchildren. *Visual Arts Research, 18*(2), 82–92.

Keyes, D. (1993). *Andree Ruellan.* Athens, GA: University of Georgia Press.

Walsh-Piper, K. (1994). Art museums and children in the United States. *NAEA Advisory.* Reston, VA: National Art Education Association.

The Ups and Downs of Middle School Motivation: Balancing Stimulating Motivation With Controlling Calm

Rosalind Ragans
Emerita, Georgia Southern University

Bunyan Morris
Marvin Pittman Laboratory School, Georgia Southern University

The middle school art teacher must achieve a delicate balance between exciting motivation and calming control to create a successful art learning environment. On one hand, the teacher wants to stimulate creative thinking; on the other, the teacher needs to maintain control of the classroom so that each individual is able to produce successful work. This balance is part of the teacher's instructional style. No two art teachers will walk that delicate tightrope in exactly the same way. Each must find his or her own style of classroom management.

The following is a menu of ideas and "dos and don'ts" that we have found successful in our many years in the classroom. Select the ideas that seem to suit you and your style of classroom management, and experiment. Just remember that you always have the next class, the next six-week session, the next semester, or the next year in which to modify your style of teaching and start all over again. That is one of the wonderful things about teaching: you can learn from your mistakes and start fresh with the next group of students.

CONTROLLING THE LEARNING ENVIRONMENT

Be ready to greet the students with a smile as they enter your classroom. Don't allow yourself to get involved with materials and supplies at that time. You must take control at that moment and set the tone for the day, or you will lose the students as they become involved in discussions with each other. It is much easier to hold control than to try to regain it once chaos has begun.

Never talk down to the students. Find the line that is comfortable for you between treating them as young adults or as children. They need guidance to handle the freedom of making exploratory decisions as middle school students. They need to be given freedom gradually. Be firm in the beginning, and slowly allow them more latitude to operate under the rules by themselves. Allow the students to participate in establishing the rules for the room. Make sure they understand that these rules must be enforceable and realistic and that they must conform to the rules of the school.

If at all possible, have a listening-discussion area apart from the studio work tables where the students come to start the class. This area can be a place for quiet activities, such as videos, slide presentations, technique demonstrations, lectures, and discussions. (If you are using audio-visual materials, always check to make sure the equipment works beforehand.) This is the place where your class begins, where you take control of the group. This can also be the place where student presentations and class summaries take place. During the rest of the class period, this space can be used as a reading-study center where books and prints are made available for research. Benches arranged in a "U" shape are a good arrangement for a discussion area. Some teachers have built bleacher-like benches and arranged them so that one quarter of the room space is the listening center. Some have used an area of carpeting on which students can sit for discussions. Even though you must crowd the students or ask them to bring chairs from a workstation to a discussion center, the end result, eye contact, will enable you to exercise control of the group. You can scan the group easily and see who is paying attention. Sometimes, you can call the wandering mind back to the group by simply making eye contact. If your room is too small for a separate listening center, try placing all the tables in a horseshoe arrangement.

The focal point of the listening center should have a display area where you can present interesting visual material that pertains to the lesson you are introducing. This area can also be a place to display student work for critical discussions. Allow students who finish assignments early to go to this area for extension, enrichment, or reteaching activities.

Be enthusiastic when introducing a lesson. The students will be sensitive to your mood. If you are not excited about the assignment, how can you expect the students to care? Never introduce a studio project until you have tested the materials and procedures. Even if you taught the same project last year, the chemical make-up of the materials may have changed, and the end results may be affected.

Even though art activities create disarray, the art room must be well organized. If you establish an orderly, attractive environment, the students will, with a little guidance, help you maintain order. Since the visual environment is an important consideration in art education, the art room itself should set an aesthetic example; it should be functional, orderly, and visually pleasing. Organize art supplies and place them on shelves where they can be reached easily. Label the shelves so that students can return the materials to the proper place at the end of each work period.

Try to provide motivation for the job of cleaning up. Some teachers have found it useful to appoint one or two students per lesson to oversee the return of materials to storage places and then assign points based on the room's degree of neatness. The student monitors do not have to put the supplies away, but they should supervise the cleanup so that you will be free to bring the lesson to closure. If the students have assigned seats, the monitors can use your seating chart to identify those who did not put away supplies or clean work areas or either. A seating chart also helps you learn names and keep order. Change the seating periodically.

Keep a notebook for substitute teachers and include plans for emergency lessons that do not require elaborate materials. Of course, if you know you are going to be absent ahead of time, you can write plans for that specific day. The substitute may not be a trained art teacher, and the students may tend to abuse supplies when you are not there. The notebook should also have seating charts for all your classes. You might indicate one or two reliable students in each class who would be helpful assistants. Information on emergency procedures should also be included in the book.

Making the art room interesting and aesthetically pleasing is as important as keeping it orderly. Try to keep a variety of live plants in your room. Not only will they enhance the visual environment, but they will be useful during various activities. Select plants that are hardy, but try to find some with different leaf shapes and sizes. If your room has no windows, invest in a grow light under which you can place the plants occasionally. Collect dried plant material and arrange it in interesting containers. Visit garage sales to find objects with interesting shapes. A piece of junk may be a treasure in a still life arrangement.

Cover the bulletin boards with inexpensive fabrics. They do not fade like paper. Try to reserve one bulletin board or display area for the students to display work done outside of class or for articles which they think will interest other students. Instead of keeping an odd assortment of cardboard boxes around the room, invest in decorative adhesive papers to cover them or paint the boxes in a pleasing color scheme.

The art room should have a logical flow to facilitate the movement of students and teachers. Be sure that work areas are not so crowded that you are unable to reach students while they are working. Use peripheral vision as the students are working. As you stop to talk to one student, be aware of the other activity in the room. You must see what the students don't think you are seeing. Don't sit down behind a desk; keep moving around the room during production activities.

If it is possible, set up a corner of the room that is the teacher's mini-studio, a place where you can produce art during free periods or after-school. It is important that the students realize that the art teacher is a producing artist and that art is an important part of your life.

The art room should have a logical flow to facilitate the movement of students and teachers.

MOTIVATION

Make the subject matter relevant to other subjects in school and to real life. Do not ask the students to draw a bunch of faded, plastic flowers. Footballs, bikes, baseball bats, radios, and shoes are so easily available and much more interesting to draw. Announce ahead of time that you are going to be setting up a still life arrangement, and ask the students to bring in objects for the arrangement that they would like to draw. Then, if possible, let the students help in setting up the arrangement. Students also like to make designs with their own names and initials. Let them solve concept problems using the shapes of letters as a basis for design.

Try to coordinate your lessons with other subject areas. For example, if the students are studying prehistory in social studies, teach them about ancient cave art, using earth pigments. Stay up to date on current trends, fads, and fashions so that you can relate the subject matter of the lesson to things in which the students are currently interested. Whether you like it or not, you need to know what kind of music they listen to, the TV shows they watch, and the movies and concerts they attend. Use the interests of the students to motivate them toward the art you want them to understand and appreciate. For example, students could use the rhythm of rap lyrics to illustrate the use of visual rhythm.

One successful way to have students participate in figure drawing is to set a schedule of birthday drawings. Stop everything for a student's birthday, and instead of cake or the usual "junk" food, hold a drawing party. The birthday person is the one who poses. Days before the event, plan a costume and props with the student. The more outrageous the costume and props, the more willing his or her friends will be to draw the model. Keeping a collection of weird outfits, hats, and props that can be found at garage sales will assist in this project. Sometimes, the birthday drawing is so interesting that classmates may decide to develop it into a finished composition. Sometimes, the model wants to keep the drawings. However, this posing must be entirely voluntary. No student should be forced to be a model for the class, and no explanation should ever be asked of the refusing student.

Take the students to a different locale to do observation drawing, if possible. Give them very specific directions, especially when working outdoors, such as: "Start with the bud at the end of the branch and work back toward the larger limbs," or "Make a circle with a piece of yarn on the ground and draw everything within the circle," or, in the lunchroom, "Start with the bottom of one chair, draw the chair, and then draw everything touching the chair until you have filled the paper."

If you can take the students to a museum, prepare them ahead of time for the visit by explaining what they are going to see and giving them information about the artists. Have a specific assignment for them to carry out at the museum. Bring art criticism study sheets and

One successful way to have students participate in figure drawing is to set a schedule of birthday drawings.

pencils. Let the students sit on the floor and write an art critique of a work they choose to study. When they return to class, have them read their descriptions, and let the other students try to identify the work.

If you cannot take the students to museums or galleries, bring original art to your class. Even the smallest rural town has "Sunday painters," folk artists, and craftspeople. Invite the artist to your class to demonstrate how he or she works. Even though you might be able to teach the same activity, middle school students are highly motivated by a "guest artist."

When holding class discussions of work in progress or final critiques, always guide the discussion with specific leading questions. Don't ever ask, "Which do you like the most?" Students will then answer according to friendship and popularity. Base your questions on the objectives of the assignment. For example: "How many shading techniques did John use in his landscape?", "Which of the slabs are decorated with high relief and which ones have used low relief?", "Which elements did Twanda use to create the feeling of excitement in her work?", or "Which elements were repeated in Leah's painting to create a rhythmic feeling?"

Once you have taught procedures for verbal activities such as art criticism and art history, arrange the students in small groups for cooperative learning activities. When the group has finished the assignment, it can present its findings to the total class. For example, if paintings or sculpture feature human figures, the group can pose in the positions of the people in the work, and then act out what they think might happen next.

When having students make art history presentations, encourage them to role-play events in the life of the artist rather than write a traditional report. Check the information for accuracy before the presentation, and offer suggestions to encourage creative thinking. Other ideas for non-traditional presentations might include writing a script about an important event in the life of the artist, writing a news interview of the artist, role-playing a TV interview of the artist, writing an art critic's review of the artist's exhibit, or creating a personal interpretation of one of the artist's famous works.

We have presented these ideas because they are teaching strategies which we have found to be successful in our personal teaching experiences with middle schoolers throughout the years. They are offered to you with the understanding that you will adapt them to your personal style of teaching.

We have presented these ideas because they are teaching strategies which we have found to be successful in our personal teaching experiences with middle schoolers throughout the years.

Instilling Confidence in Middle School Students Through Intelligent Grid Drawing Assignments

INTRODUCTION

Carol Susann Stavropoulos
University of Georgia

Few will disagree that middle school children often lack confidence and are critical of their own artistic endeavors (Lowenfeld & Brittain, 1987; Burton, 1981; Moody, 1992). However, according to the National Art Education Association's *Art Education: Middle/Junior High School* (NAEA, 1979), "the young adolescent generally has a high degree of manipulative ability and a keen interest in developing technical skills" (p. 104). Grid drawing can help adolescents learn techniques of shading, and is also an effective way to arrive at more accurate proportions (Anderson, 1979; Hubbard, 1986a). According to Anderson, "as a method of convincing students that they can, indeed, draw a straight line and as a way of building self-confidence . . . . the gridded drawing method is a most effective tool" (p. 34). Anderson provides instructions and results of this method, emphasizing the use of a grid to reproduce a photographic image.

Too often, the lessons learned from grid drawing are limited to discriminating values, measurement, hand-eye coordination, and self-discipline. These outcomes are valid and appropriate in the middle school art program where teaching objectives include developing technical skill and confidence in drawing. While techniques are tools to more effective expression, Hathaway (NAEA, 1979) warns that "techniques should never become ends in themselves, and the art program should never be built around technical facility alone" (p. 104).

There are numerous accounts in the art education literature focusing on levels of confidence as essential to continued attempts to draw, with titles ranging from "*I Can't Draw!*" (Reynard, 1971) to "*I Can Draw!*" (Hart, 1988). Other scholarly articles (Pariser, 1979; Smith, 1985; Robertson, 1987) explore the topic of copying in terms

Art production must extend beyond the mere acquisition of technical skills—providing students opportunities to think, solve problems, and to express their own imaginative ideas.

of the development of self-confidence. For some time, grid drawing has been used by art teachers as a vehicle to develop students' confidence in drawing. Art lessons related to grid drawing appear in several middle school art textbooks (Hubbard, 1986a, 1986b; Chapman, 1987) and in current resources on teaching drawing (Cikanova, 1992; Burger & Ragouzis, 1993), and design (Gatto, Porter, & Selleck, 1987).

The advantages and disadvantages of copying and mechanical drawing have been previously analyzed in great depth by Duncam (1988). This chapter, through the documentation of one student's success, will demonstrate how grid drawing extends beyond direct copying, assists middle school students in mastering necessary technical skills, and helps them develop a sense of self-confidence and pride. Furthermore, ideas will be offered for enriching the learning experience gained through grid drawing.

ONE ART TEACHER'S ACCOUNT OF THE VALUE OF GRID DRAWING: DOUG'S STORY

"Essential virtues for the middle school art teacher are patience, structure, enthusiam, and a genuine concern for the adolescent. The growth and development middle school students experience through appropriate art activities can enhance their confidence and instill a sense of trust in themselves and others." (Nancy Vanderbreek Elliott, Art Specialist, Burney-Harris-Lions Middle School, Athens, Georgia.)

Looking back to when I was fresh out of student teaching, I remember wondering, will I survive my first trimester at a middle school?" It was to my advantage to work with the previous art teacher who, at mid-year, had been promoted to Vice-Principal. I observed the first few days during the transition. She was teaching grid drawing methods to eighth-grade art students. She shared her bag of tricks with me (how to accurately copy the difficult shadows around the nose, the secret to drawing hair, the use of reflections and highlights, etc.). She also, in no uncertain terms, informed me that the art program was well recognized for the photographic grid drawings her students produced, and I was expected to enter work of this caliber in various local, state, and national art competitions. However, the production of slick images solely for the purposes of art contests clearly did not bear the students' best interests in mind (Blair, 1995). Further, grid drawing of this nature went against everything I had been taught in my teacher training program. Art production must extend beyond the mere acquisition of technical skills—providing students opportunities to think, solve problems, and to express their own imaginative ideas. Could grid drawing meet this criteria? I was soon to find out.

Doug came into my seventh-grade classroom—slicked-back hair, black leather jacket, ripped-up jeans, T-shirt—with the stride of a tough guy. Doug would not be satisfied in the role of ordinary middle school student; it was his intention, I assumed, to turn my class upside-down on his first day back from in-school suspension. Of course, he lived up to my expectations, refusing to do the assignments, roaming about the room, and talking back to me in front of the other students.

As a new teacher, I was appalled. I tried to correct his behavior on several occasions. His response was to avoid eye contact and to look downward; he paid no attention to my reprimands and turned his back on me. Although he was rough, tough, and belligerent, Doug displayed a certain vulnerability when he looked down at that cold cement floor. He made me feel as if I had just corrected a rambunctious puppy tearing into a 20-pound bag of kitty litter, the pup not really understanding what he had done to cause my disapproval. When I finished letting Doug know how I would not tolerate such rudeness, he looked at me with puppy dog eyes. His sad expression touched me, and I knew at that moment I had failed miserably in relating and communicating with Doug. I then became determined to find a way to reach him.

In-school suspension was a way of life for Doug, as he did not care at all about classroom rules and consequences. However, by making him an occasional classroom assistant, my relationship with Doug became more positive, and his behavior in class improved.

Doug had been back in class for only a week and a half when I received a notice that he would be serving another in-school suspension sentence beginning the next week. I was instructed to prepare a week's worth of class assignments for him to complete during that time.

One afternoon Doug stayed after school to help me hang the finished eighth-grade grid drawings. Admiring the realistic drawings, Doug indicated that he would like to see "a Harley motorcycle drawn like that!" I remarked, "Bring in a picture of one, and I'll show you how to do it." But Doug uttered the typical declaration, "I can't draw!"

Before the start of school the very next day, however, Doug brought a Harley motorcycle magazine into the classroom. He told me that he wanted to work on the drawing during in-school suspension. Such a drawing was at least a week's work, so I quickly helped him measure and lay out the grid. He attached this grid-lined paper onto a protective sheet of posterboard and made a cover out of tracing paper. I instructed Doug to return to the art room during my planning period. In-school suspension personnel complied with my request, sending Doug down to the art room at the appointed time. Doug had already been introduced to contour drawing; his assignment had been to draw his hands and shoes. Now, concentrating on one square at a time, I showed him how to find contour lines within each square of the grid format. First, he worked in the basic contour lines and shapes, and then he smudged in the values with a cotton swab. Doug went back to in-school suspension for the rest of the day

In-school suspension was a way of life for Doug, as he did not care at all about classroom rules and consequences.

with his viewfinder, protected drawing paper, and Harley magazine. He came by my room after school eager to show me his progress. Doug had successfully completed four 1-inch by 1-inch (2.54-cm) sections of what appeared to be reflective metal exhaust pipes. While there was still a great deal more work ahead, he had begun to grasp the technique.

The next day, the in-school suspension teacher came to my room. She exclaimed, "I've never seen anything like it! In all the days Doug has been in in-school suspension, I have never seen him pick up a pencil! And now, he won't put it down!"

When Doug finished his Harley, I framed it with black posterboard and covered it with acetate, just like the other grid drawings Doug had admired. It wasn't perfect craftsmanship by any means; the paper was slightly torn in one corner, and there were some bends in the surface where he had leaned so intently against it as he worked. However, you could without question discern the shiny Harley Davidson!

Since this drawing was a major accomplishment for Doug, special recognition was in order. I devoted a central bulletin board in the front of the room to the work and spelled out Doug's name with silver letters. Students in Doug's class sincerely complimented him on his drawing, and each day Doug brought in a different teacher to admire it. Even the Principal made a special trip to see the Harley. Long overdue, the positive feedback Doug received made him stand very tall indeed.

This story illustrates how grid drawing made a difference in one student's life. There is no doubt that Doug developed self-confidence in his drawing ability with the grid drawing method. He also experienced pride in his accomplishment and a sense of self-worth changing his entire attitude and demeanor for the better.

OTHER SKILLS THAT CAN BE TAUGHT THROUGH GRID DRAWING

In broadening the grid drawing experience beyond technique, Anderson (1979) addressed the importance of teaching students about artists throughout history. For instance, Leonardo da Vinci, Dürer, and Michelangelo relied upon grid techniques to create great works of art (Gardner, de la Croix, & Tansey, 1970; Burger & Ragouzis, 1993). Fernand Léger applied the grid in creating precise Cubist renditions of still life images (Januszczak, 1982). Mark Chagall also incorporated a loosely drawn grid to translate a preparatory sketch of *The Birthday* onto canvas (Compton, 1985).

There are many contemporary artists who utilize a grid in producing their works. Photorealists such as Chuck Close and Richard Estes have applied grid methods to create surprisingly realistic works of art from photographs. The result of Close's tedious efforts are gigantic portraits that resemble illustrations from contemporary magazines. Audrey Flack has also employed grid methods by projecting a slide

Students in Doug's class sincerely complimented him on his drawing, and each day Doug brought in a different teacher to admire it.

onto the canvas and then painting in one area at a time (Kurtz, 1987). Muralists also depend on grid methods when enlarging and painting supergraphics onto large walls and buildings (Greenburg, Smith, & Teacher, 1977).

BEYOND COPYING

There are ways to use creatively a grid-drawing technique beyond simply that of reproducing an image. Distortion grids, collages, and selective breakdowns of the image being drawn are all techniques of grid drawing which can be used by students to transform an image and represent it in a new way.

Distortion grids

Roukes (1982) suggested altering images through the use of distortion grids which transform the proportions of images. A regular grid of squares is placed on the image to be transformed, and the same number of rectangles are arranged in a grid on the drawing paper. It is important that the grid of rectangles have the same number of vertical and horizontal lines as the grid of squares on the image to be drawn. However, rectangles on the drawing paper have to vary in proportion from the original grid, causing the distortion. Each segment of the grid-covered image is transferred to the corresponding segment of the grid of rectangles. When the segments of the image in the grid squares are transposed into rectangular shapes, the image is stretched either horizontally or vertically. The degree to which the image is stretched is dependent on the size of the rectangles plotted on the drawing paper (e.g., a 1-in. x 3-in. [2.34-cm x 6.02-cm] rectangle will stretch the image more than a 1-in. x 2-in. [2.34-cm x 4.68-cm] rectangle). Roukes also proposed transposing an image onto a diamond-shaped grid with vanishing points at the top and bottom or onto a grid that resembles a zigzag polygon arrangement.

Collage

A collage project utilizing portions of grid drawing in combination with actual magazine images was developed when a student became so dissatisfied with the background of her grid drawing that she gave up and threw it into the trash can. I retrieved the drawing and pointed out the salvageable areas that were rendered quite well. She cut out the female figure with a tousled head of hair, looking downward, and discarded the background area, which she did not like. Focusing on the unusual pose and evasiveness of the figure helped her decide that the figure needed a stormy background. She then searched through old *National Geographic* and *Smithsonian* magazines and found photographs of various weather conditions. She collaged a stormy sea, dark sunset, and angry cloud formation

There are ways to creatively use a grid-drawing technique beyond simply that of reproducing an image.

Even when technique is emphasized, grid drawing can help students experience feelings of success and confidence, as was described in Doug's story.

behind her grid drawing of the figure onto a sheet of black matte board. The student also used a white colored pencil to draw her own interpretations of cloud formations on areas of the black matte board.

Students can also create collages by arranging a variety of magazine and newspaper images into one composition. My middle school students came up with themes such as flying, anger, death, and love. They then applied a grid to the original collage, and either enlarged, reduced, or distorted the composition on the drawing paper. Color can be added for emphasis.

Selective breakdown of the image

Rather than copying every grid segment of the image, students can selectively leave some segments blank. For instance, a student created a grid drawing from a photograph of Buffalo Bill but left blank the grid areas that enclosed the eyes. One could ask whether the eyes were left out intentionally, and if so, what kind of statement was made. It was intriguing how easily the subject of the portrait could be identified despite the empty segments.

CONCLUSION

Even when technique is emphasized, grid drawing can help students experience feelings of success and confidence, as was described in Doug's story. However, confidence can also be instilled in middle school students through grid drawing assignments that encourage further learning, thinking, and imagination. Distortion grids, collages, and selective breakdown of images are only a few ways to extend grid methods beyond technique and direct copying.

The author encourages middle school art educators to develop grid drawing assignments that allow images to be rendered in new, original ways and that encourage students to think about the meanings projected in the grid drawings they create. Further, it is suggested that such art activities be taught in conjunction with studies of artists, both past and present, who have employed grid methods in creating works of art.

REFERENCES

Anderson, T. (1979). Gridded drawings. *School Arts, 79*(1), 34–35.

Blair, L. (1995). The critical eye: Art contests from one judge's perspective. *Art Education, 48*(1), 62–65.

Burger, T. S., & Ragouzis, P. N. (1993). Dürergrid: An old idea revisited. *School Arts, 93*(1), 26–27.

Burton, J. M. (1981). Representing experiences: Ideas in search of form. *School Arts, 80* (5), 58–64.

Cikanova, K. (1992). *Teaching children to draw*. New York: Craftsman House.

Chapman, L. H. (1987). *Discover art: Grades 1–6*. Worcester, MA: Davis Publications.

Compton, S. (1985). *Chagall*. New York: Harry N. Abrams.

Duncum, P. (1988). To copy or not to copy: A review. *Studies in Art Education, 29*(4), 203–210.

Gatto, J. A., Porter, A. W., & Selleck, J. (1987). *Exploring visual design*. Worcester, MA: Davis Publications.

Greenburg, D., Smith, K., & Teacher, S. (1977). *Megamurals and supergraphics: Big art*. Philadelphia: Running Press.

Hart, K. (1988). *I can draw! Ideas for teachers*. Portsmouth, NH: Heinemann.

Gardner, H., de la Croix, H., & Tansey, R. G. (1970). *Art through the ages* (rev. ed.). New York: Harcourt, Brace, & World.

Hubbard, G. (1986a). *Art in Action: Grade 7*. San Diego: Coronado Publishers.

Hubbard, G. (1986b). *Art in Action: Grade 8*. San Diego: Coronado Publishers.

Januszczak, W. (1982). *Techniques of the world's great painters*. Secaucus, NJ: Chartwell Books.

Kurtz, B. D. (1987). *Visual imagination: An introduction to art*. Englewood Cliffs, NJ: Prentice-Hall.

Lowenfeld, V., & Brittain, W. L. (1987). *Creative and mental growth*. New York: Macmillan.

Moody, L. J. (1992). An analysis of drawing programs for early adolescents. *Studies in Art Education, 34*(1), 39–47.

National Art Education Association. (1979). *Art education: Middle/junior high school*. Walter Hathaway (Task force chairman). Reston, VA: The National Art Education Association.

Pariser, D. A. (1979). Two methods of teaching drawing skills. *Studies in Art Education, 20*(3), 30–42.

Reynard, C. C. (1971). I can't draw. *School Arts, 71*(3), 48–49.

Robertson, A. (1987) Borrowing and artistic behavior: A case-study of the development of Bruce's spontaneous drawings from six to sixteen. *Studies in Art Education, 29*(1), 37–51.

Roukes, N. (1982). *Art synectics*. Worcester, MA: Davis Publications.

Smith, N. R. (1985). Copying and artistic behaviors: Children and comic strips. *Studies in Art Education, 26*(3), 147–156.

Exploring Art in Middle School

George Szekely
University of Kentucky

What is between childhood art and the elective art classes of high school? Middle school art experiences should be a significant bridge between elementary and high school art, but it is the preparation for high school art that is most commonly emphasized. What is offered today in many schools are teacher-invented studio projects and a sampling of art history as preparation for departmentalized high school studio programs. Under courses entitled "Exploratory Art," a journey usually takes place through known art techniques from shading to perspective. Instead of old ways of making, looking at, and thinking about art, exploratory courses could examine the nature of art-making and teach students how to discover art. These courses should stimulate independent thinking and open students' eyes to art in their own lives and in the environment. Middle school students can learn how to conduct artistic investigations and to collect and utilize observations and experiences as sources for art. The artist can be presented as an innovator, the art process as invention, and the art class as a research site. No matter how the art world changes, we should seek basic understandings that are timeless.

Exploring Art is the name of a demonstration project funded to study the effects of the above philosophy and place it into school practice. Now in its fourth year, the project has served over 450 students in the central Kentucky schools. A four-week summer course offered at the University of Kentucky was designed to explore with teachers new approaches to middle school art teaching. The session generates a sign-up list of enthusiastic (sometimes skeptical) teachers willing to participate the following year. Our project works with all students on the host teacher's schedules. The project is guided by the philosophy of Marcel Duchamp, whose work revolutionized contemporary conceptions of art, and who might well have said, "Don't only look for art in art, but search everywhere." Our middle school students seek art in their pockets and in their backyards. They look for art in primary sources, not just in museums and adult interpretations. They become scouts of the world, using hobbies, travels, chores, and social occasions to draw awareness of art possibilities.

Future artists will have to be explorers. They need to learn early to be resourceful and imaginative in finding and making art, to learn that everything has art possibilities and can be auditioned for art uses. Children who through playful exploration invented much of what is "new" on the contemporary art scene should not be stifled in later years. Their inventive art spirits need preservation during the middle school years. Instead of art classes that only tell about art, placing boundaries on its processes, art teaching has to be viewed as an opening of possibilities, a way to see through the widest perspective. Teaching art is the preservation of the essential artist within us all. Art can keep playful hands occupied and spirits intact, exercise collecting instincts and nurture the appreciation of interesting objects in all aspects of life, and place value on those things made by hand. Students can learn to rely on themselves as designers and creators of objects and ideas and to be confident in their personal choices as they look at their own lives for playful and creative possibilities. Students maintain notebooks of personal observations and "Idea Books" in addition to school notebooks which are typically used to record the ideas of others. They learn to value their own finds as they learn about objects and events of significance to one another. Writing and sketching, describing personal observations, and diagramming inventions can all become second nature. Our students learn to take notes on everything and to collect from everywhere.

During the middle school years, there is great pressure to grow up. Students typically enter departmentalized programs and encounter teachers who encourage them to make adult judgments, to develop adult learning styles, and, of course, to make adult art. At home, toys are thrown away, and rooms often are purged of fun "stuff." The demands on the adolescent's time increases, reducing the time needed for independent thinking, being alone, or simply having creative fun. Seldom on the schedule is time to develop qualities important to becoming an artist, such as self-reliance, or the time needed for creative dreaming and using one's own ideas and research abilities. Young children are full-time creative investigators, and art is close to their lives, present in their play and in their interests. By middle school, art has become a subject based on ideas and skills formulated by others and is often estranged from children's natural creative styles.

What happens to the creative house, store, and restaurant players of childhood in middle school? Children who invented new worlds, objects, and environments and set up everything as a great display at home come to school and say they have no ideas. It is these home players—the ones who can design all spaces, animate all objects, and design any new product—who need support. In our middle school art class, we frequently call ourselves "a design company." We continue to play house; for example, but students are challenged to think like designers and architects and redesign objects and places.

The design of Exploring Art was based on a desire to preserve the following characteristics of childhood artists:

- Elementary age children make art any time with anything. Middle school students typically wait for art, wait for instructions, and wait for supplies and assignments. In our program, students are encouraged to seek art in personal experiences, daily acts, and the environment.

- Young children pick up things; they discover beauty in unsuspected objects and save favorite "treasures." Their search for art is active, taking place during walks, bike rides, or store visits. We work to maintain art as a full-time activity, to make it a part of everyone's life. Art is presented as an investigation and a discovery instead of a following of techniques distilled by others.

- Young children tend to be interested in everything they see, from antiques to the latest in designed objects to intricate forms in nature. Middle schoolers have begun to narrow their worlds of interest and are less likely to look around freely or browse for extended periods of time. We work to recapture a sense of freedom to play with objects; to touch, try out, and try on things; to build with everything; and to rekindle the appreciation of environmental offerings.

- Young children feel they can make anything. They look to themselves for ideas with confidence and are proud of the things they make. In later school years, students believe that what others make is better and that all has been found and explored. Middle school experiences have to rebuild the students' confidence in their abilities as visual explorers and innovators.

- Young children can't wait for art supplies as they convert, reshape, and re-imagine objects they encounter. Middle school students learn to have a more definite idea of what an art material is as well as what art is and what it is not. They are reluctant to work without official supplies or in areas outside of what is understood to be art. We need to offer a broader view of the art world that can expand everyone's art supply and activity lists.

- Young children find possibilities for creation in simple chores and everyday tasks while older students see these activities as merely work and routines. We teach middle schoolers how to "jam" again; to make music without notes, to put things together without instruction sheets, to take things apart without fear, and to explore their world without adult blueprints.

- Children express their own feelings, dreams, and wishes through their art. Middle schoolers are more reluctant to express such personal feelings and thoughts in art. In our teaching, we remind them that they still have ideas and significant contributions to

Children express their own feelings, dreams, and wishes through their art.

make and that their personal feelings and observations on their life experiences can be valuable art sources.

- Young children feel like artists. By middle school, everyone knows who the "real" class artists are—those who can copy accurately cartoon characters, and so on. We work to broaden middle schoolers' perceptions of the artist as someone with vision, an inventor, and an idea person, in essence, someone who can discover art. We need to help them recognize the artist within themselves.

MAINTENANCE OF THE PERFORMANCE ARTIST

Middle school students no longer feel free to take part in some childhood activities; they know they're "too old" to go "trick or treating" anymore. Those were the days—when they pretended they were something else and stayed up late to arrange and display their candies. It is not that middle schoolers wouldn't like to dress up in costumes or don't envy the smell of fresh makeup smeared across a younger sibling's face. Children don't suddenly stop enjoying the pleasures of dressing up and performing in their own costume creations, but they certainly lack opportunities as they get older. Home closets don't stay open indefinitely as adults become less generous in lending clothes, and the desire to appear more grown-up keeps teenagers from engaging in such creative fun.

At school, the art room can serve as the dressing room of rock stars or circus performers. Selections of vintage clothes, old hats, Hawaiian shirts, and wild ties provide opportunities to use the body as canvas and to stage a variety of showings. We are all a canvas on which we arrange colors and patterns and continue to express moving talents. In Exploring Art, students arrange store windows and flowers and model landscapes for Hollywood as a means for active designing. While most middle school classes focus on the transferal of information, students in the art class continue to manipulate objects and experiment with costumes. They learn that an artist should never forget how to engage in creative play and that play can be the source of important ideas.

MAINTAINING A PLAYFUL REACH INTO THE ENVIRONMENT

Sharing my cylindrical Legos, circa 1948, with sixth graders caused them to recall their favorite childhood blocks and other objects they used to "make things with." Pillow mountains, encyclopedia highways, clothes-pin people, foil animals, and box mansions were all talked about with excitement. Students can learn through such discussion the value of their past creative experiences and how these experiences can be stepping stones to future artistic expression. The ability to take stock of the creative possibility in ordinary objects requires

We are all a canvas on which we arrange colors and patterns and continue to express moving talents.

lifelong practice. A daily classroom search demonstrates that everything can have an art use. The students build with anything—from rulers and erasers to umbrellas brought in during a rain. Staplers have become Star Wars explorers in student animations. Books and chairs have been turned into bridges, buildings, and displays. In other places, there are few opportunities to creatively "play" with the environment. In the art class, all objects can be touched, handled, juggled, animated, and altered; active curiosity is encouraged as we promote curious hands and the minds that follow.

MAINTAINING INTEREST IN ART OCCASIONS

Middle schoolers enjoy social events, forgetting the art occasions they used to be. Guest lists become artworks in the decorative hands of young party planners. The "countdown" calendar evolves into a beautiful wall piece as days are crossed-out daily. Student-wrapped presents and hand-made invitations become part of the artwork. Children are never too old to design their own events and create special occasions. Middle schoolers have little opportunity to get involved in such pleasures at home; the art room can become a place where they can be actively involved. Through party plans, students learn to place value on handmade sculptural art such as gift wrapping and place settings. To make our classroom spaces festive and exciting requires continuous practice. Students beautify presents, rooms, and even themselves as they learn about art as an offering to someone special.

MAINTAINING FULL-TIME ARTISTS

"It's Karp!" my younger daughter exclaims with excitement sharing the pictures she made during a cello recital. Young children function as artists naturally; whereas, middle schoolers hesitate to make their art in public. We believe that the most important learning beyond the early years is that which empowers students to make art everywhere and always. Young children set up "art" studios everywhere and create art occasions from all aspects of life. Older students function less as artists outside of an art class; instead, they make art in response to someone else's assigned tasks. After all, art teachers who assign projects have the ideas. Students come to feel less confident of art as an ability we all share which can be called upon at all times. When art is restored as a regular part of the students' experiences, they begin to see and feel again where art ideas can come from, sensing their own abilities to generate ideas and a confidence to share and teach them to others.

We place sketchbooks in every pocket and on every night table to record dreams and reactions to special events. Students examine how they can interrupt routines and incorporate art into their daily activi-

We place sketchbooks in every pocket and on every night table to record dreams and reactions to special events.

ties. For example, students chauffeured and bussed to school and other activities rename the vehicles "mobile studios." They become aware of the unique views and opportunities to make art on a moving bus or van. In art diaries, they make visual notes to tell about themselves and their lives and to record their observations. (Our lunch box diaries, sketchbooks in a box, may not be famous—yet.) They study the writings of Mark Twain, Anne Frank, and the visual diaries of the photographer Lartigue, the painter Matisse, and the architect Le Corbusier.

MAINTAINING INTEREST IN THE ARTS OF ONE'S LIFE

Young children create sculpture from pencil shavings and foil found in the kitchen. Home is the central place for art as children animate their combs and brushes and make them dance to the background noise of television commercials. They borrow from all sources utilizing movement and surrounding sounds in a lively blend of sculpture, dances, cheers, and hand claps.

Middle schoolers often take lessons after school to study drama, guitar, ballet, or tap. We survey our students who participate in such creative rehearsals for sports, music, or dance. Even though their creative activities become specialized and are learned in organized programs, we use them as models for art sources. Everyone is asked to observe the creative movement possibilities in these activities: for example, how batons or bats are held or how arms, toes, and bodies are moved. The students survey the visual qualities and the sounds or feel of each activity and apply their discoveries to imaginary drawing tools or painting motions: drum sticks with art tool attachments, shoes with crayons attached to the soles or to skates, and drawing tools that dance or strum across art stages. An "instrumentalist" holds the page like a cello and bows across it in experimental sketches. Students gain new ways of viewing, holding, and moving across art surfaces through the study of these after-school activities. Different practicing and rehearsal styles are compared, and the diaries, musical scores, game plans, and choreographers' diagrams are studied as visual sketchbooks. After-school life can be linked to artistic life, providing opportunities for new visual works.

MAINTAINING THE WONDER OF ART IN DAILY EVENTS

Parents will tell you of the eternity it takes for young children to get ready in the morning; it may be because their preparation borders on art. They play in the bathroom, pulling down toilet paper to make faces on the floor. Toothpaste is squeezed into drawings on a shiny sink. Soap and sponges are played with in the tub. Getting dressed means reviewing a vast palette of colors and patterns. Breakfast is

Home is the central place for art as children animate their combs and brushes and make them dance to the background noise of television commercials.

filled with design opportunities as cocoa or butter faces are made on a hot, white canvas of cereal.

Middle schoolers feel restrained from participating in such creative opportunities. In class, we examine the rich sources of art that are still present in their daily lives. Middle schoolers, for example, spend a considerable amount of time combing their hair. We encourage playful styling; we think of hair notions like curlers and combs as sculpture materials. Students examine historic and tribal hair styles in visual arts history and create hair substitutes made of cotton candy, foils and tennis balls. Adolescents, who generally are interested in food preparation, can regain the right to play in the kitchen, which used to be a prime home art space. They study table setting as an art form and cake decorating as painting and sculpture. They look at the history of soup bowls, pitchers, china, and dinnerware. We take stock of small kitchen appliances as potential art tools: the toaster as canvas-maker, the popcorn-maker as sculpture designer, and the blender as paint mixer.

MAINTAINING THE ART IN HOME CHORES

When children are young, they are eager to help. After all, sweeping is just drawing; mopping is painting; and a rake is another sculpture tool for making monsters or houses out of leaves with individual rooms set out on the lawn. When something needs fixing under the hood of the car or inside an appliance, young children are there to enjoy the taking apart and sculptural act of rebuilding. If a bike or a steel shelf purchase comes in a thousand parts, children are the only ones who welcome that challenge. When children get older, the question becomes, "How much money will I get if I help?" Chores are tied to allowances and to work; they are to be done efficiently and fast, not creatively. Work comes to stand apart from being creative. In the art class, students use screw drivers to look inside computers or old clocks. They put together shelves in extraordinary ways and rake playfully. We recapture the joys of rummaging inside a tool box and rediscover the playfulness in polishing or watering as drawing or hammering as sculpture. All hand tools are redefined as art tools. As an introduction to future arts, we explore familiar sources and childhood experiences.

MAINTAINING INTEREST IN CHANGE

You cannot move one item out of a young child's room without the child noticing it. Children enjoy decorating their personal spaces, changing them daily, moving things about, or displaying new items on the door, over the television set, or above the sink. Personal bulletin boards and desk tops and drawers receive a great deal of design

When children get older, the question becomes, "How much money will I get if I help?"

The confident and sensitive descriptions of media, process, and design demonstrate a close study of the collection and a solid foundation for the appreciation of portrait painting and sculpture.

attention. Spaces are used for setups and displays. Redecorating is continually in progress.

We need to maintain licensed room designers by offering spaces for middle schoolers to remodel and create private displays. We recount every renovation project, such as room additions, as well as neighborhood designs for preservation or the construction of a new shopping center. Young children are excited about pocketing samples of building materials or saving scrap siding or countertop pieces they like. In middle school, our students envision changes and plan along with the adult designers, drawing up plans, looking through lighting catalogs, and visiting building suppliers. Each renovation, of course, yields exciting drawing and painting surfaces on which to experiment, from bricks to ceiling tiles to insulation boards. The students continue to plan and dream through doll houses, which we now call *models*, and create contemporary furnishings or new ideas for phones and appliances in the roles of industrial designers. The students study the historic sculpture of old phones and doll house kitchens as examples. Children's outdoor landscaping play is continued as they create rock gardens and landscaping plans for school yard plots.

MAINTAINING INTEREST IN OLD THINGS

I share a beautiful Superman lunch box with my eighth graders, a prize I recently found at a flea market. We look at a catalog of old lunch boxes and survey the current styles in class. A love for the old (toys, tops, teddy bears, and doll houses) is a strong foundation for the love of art history. Young children eagerly collect buttons, marbles, or baseball cards. They are willing to view the history of drawing and painting along with the history of their favorite objects. Middle schoolers' pockets are empty in comparison, and they often speak with sadness of the "stuff" that was thrown out or that they used to have. After realizing how students still value collections, we rekindle an interest in toy box affairs. Students look at fashion history through the Barbie doll or at architectural styles through doll houses. Equally important, we try to build new areas of collecting for each student. Collectors develop an expertise in a visual arts area. We recognize unofficial collections and support the "start up" of new ones. Many students have not considered their saved items being related to art as we help make connections using the many collectors' books now available on just about any subject. We support the re-examination of homes, our first "museums"; reaching deeply into trunks and attics to share and discuss individual finds from old postcards (architectural and printed history), old scarves and handkerchiefs (American geometric art), or old stamps (portraiture). We listen to presentations of collections as we build confidence and pride in new art interests. Just listen to a young baseball card collector of early twentieth century cards explaining posing techniques or lighting and printing procedures used in printed portraits. The confident and sensitive descriptions of media, process, and design demonstrate a close study of the collection and a solid foundation for the appreciation of portrait painting and sculpture. Students are likely to expand these interests to learn about other objects and arts.

MAINTAINING AN INTEREST IN CONTEMPORARY MATERIALS

Young children want to keep everything. As they get older, they are praised for cleaning up and throwing away things in their room and at fast-food restaurants. Saving even important treasures is not always encouraged. In the art class, we support browsing and encourage students to save things. Future artists need to be constantly on the lookout for what is new and interesting. During our Fast Food Week, for example, we visit our favorite art supply store, the local fast-food restaurant. There we find the latest in canvasses, from foam trays to sculptural containers. Paint packets come in mustard or ketchup packs. While young children instinctively pocket such supplies, our middle schoolers first stake out specific supply sites and work toward creating categories for the resources they find. The ability to see new and unusual uses for ordinary objects is not lost in later years if it is consistently exercised and rewarded. Through each search, at fast-food restaurants and other popular sites, we look for materials that are contemporary and representative of our American way of life. Students collect and sample colorful storage units or the latest in Post-it pads as we pitch ideas for their creative use and display. Each storage unit, for example, is seen as an architectural shopping center, a model for a new sports arena, or a car wash. Students learn that shopping for art is an important part of the art process as they look for new inventions in contemporary objects and materials.

The ability to see new and unusual uses for ordinary objects is not lost in later years if it is consistently exercised and rewarded.

MAINTAINING AN INTEREST IN SHOPPING

Go shopping with a young child and be ready to spend all your time looking for them. Children can get lost in any store; wandering through aisles becomes an adventure with a mission to discover what is most fun. They want everything and see objects as raw materials with which to create. They offer wonderful suggestions when asked to justify this need. Shopping stretches the artist within a child.

Middle school students are more reserved shoppers. They are more likely to stay on familiar aisles, touching objects and playing less, but are more intent on purchasing the particular thing they came in to buy. Our art class promotes shopping adventures as we turn to each aisle for art ideas. With a budget of $1.00 or $100 in Monopoly money, we examine unusual items in untraveled aisles, talking about hair curlers or oil wrenches as sculpture or drawing tools. We visit stores as a group and also shop in stores set up in class. Students take items that are free for sampling, picking up self-sticking labels, order forms, and packaging cards from the Post Office. They save tickets and receipts from gas stations and banks as they sample the contemporary world for art surfaces. The art class becomes an important place to gather collections, exchange ideas, and display unique finds. To emphasize that everything can be an art object, supply, or tool, we discuss the finder's ideas. We review the possibilities of transforming each object, how it can be changed through animation or sculptural additions. Finding time for shopping is suggested as students are encouraged to gather things found while waiting for the school bus or walking to school. Middle school students who have forgotten to look down and pick up outdoor treasures regain these artistic pleasures. There is no need to go to the moon to uncover special rocks when we have pieces of broken sidewalks or a fallen bud to collect. Each object is wrapped in possibilities as students learn to be alert and to share each shopping discovery. During holidays, we save catalogs from toys, plumbing parts, kitchen equipment, or gardening tools and find interesting art uses within each page.

MAINTAINING AN INTEREST IN MAKING THINGS BEAUTIFUL

Children decorate everything; the mail they send to friends, their school folders and notebooks, even their bandages are covered in designs. Our bathroom tiles are filled with stickers, and each switch plate is patterned with drawings. Are these instincts to beautify one's world encouraged in later years?

For middle school students, it is important to provide further opportunities to make a more beautiful environment. Our students design shopping bags and T-shirts, tablecloths and pillows to carry their decorations into the world. Everything in the art class itself can be covered—chairs, tables, floors, and walls—to make a change in the environment with the students' own imprints. Every object can be looked upon as needing improvement, as something that can be redesigned in our own version for our own purposes. Famous name-brand companies have not yet invented the most outstanding shoe; these latest styles are created in our art class and displayed in our "stores." The feeling that everything can be beautified and redesigned is a necessary realization for the future artist.

MAINTAINING CHILDREN'S INTEREST IN THE NEW

Young children are always interested in the latest products and often know about new ones before these products reach the attention of adults. During "Back to School" sales, excitement is found in the latest color of paper clips and the new graphics on pencils. The interest in the new is an important quality for future artists. Older students have produced many school projects and have been exposed to more

Children decorate everything; the mail they send to friends, their school folders and notebooks, even their bandages are covered in designs.

opinions and accepted examples of art. They learn what art is and thus form increasingly narrow views of art. What we know of the future of art today is that we don't know what art will be in our students' lifetimes. Will it be made of ice or ice cream, played through a video game, or tracked in space signals? Maintaining interest and openness to new ideas and forms from technology to all media and fields needs to be part of students' art preparation today. The art room can become the official place where all new things are brought and reviewed. With lively conversation, our students discuss exciting recent photographs from space or a new drinking straw which can be used to compose tunes by humming while drinking.

Young children anxiously await Friday's "Show and Tell," planning days ahead of time what they want to share at school. This need to have an audience, to recognize and discuss one's special finds, should be acknowledged in middle school. The ability to pick out unusual items and find pride and excitement in the process needs to be encouraged. Our middle school "Show and Tell" is focused on the future, on objects and designs that students feel are predictors of new art worlds. Students look for the latest in science magazines and in technology papers as well as in objects. For example, in our discussion of midi cellos, there is a browsing through catalogs of midi instruments and forecasting the instrumentation of midi drawing tools.

Students discuss contemporary "galleries" of the art which is printed on their pillows, towels, shower curtains, and sleeping bags. We dream of worlds beyond as students suggest art galleries with blank walls where artists come, wearing their art as watch dials or items of clothing. We look toward the future by thinking beyond the ordinary, by surveying the existing and seeing what items need to be changed and redesigned. Through these experiences, students learn that art lives in the extraordinary and that through dreams, silly talk, and active brainstorming, we can think of doing and making things differently. Our seventh graders, for example, sleep on special art pillows; our eighth graders take special art "potions" (different colored jelly beans) as they dream of extraordinary places, entering new time zones and time machines while recording images and ideas from each imaginary interlude.

EVALUATION

Student portfolios are the principal evaluation tool for the program. We are interested not only in the students' artworks, but also in the degree of artistic thinking and the ability of students to function as artists. In addition to artworks, there are several components required in each student portfolio:
1. "Art Idea Books" are expanded sketchbooks with written notations of observations, environmental finds, and plans for their use and their relationship to one's art. Some entries are suggest-

Student portfolios are the principal evaluation tool for the program.

There is a great rebuilding of students' artistic confidence in knowing that the art world has not been pre-invented for them, that their contributions and ideas are still welcome.

ed by the teacher, but many are independent inserts by students. Idea books become a place to consider art in one's life and experiences and to record reactions to shopping, travels, plays, or performance events. The idea books are used to generate ideas for artworks.

2. Student reports on events are made with an art emphasis. Events are analyzed through photographs, sketches, and writings and discussed in terms of art materials, subjects, and movements related to art. Reports on walks, school dances, home chores, birthdays, or outdoor activities are included.

3. "What Art Means To Me" is an illustrated self-study authored by every class member. Students discuss their changing art views, including the many art sources and ideas gained from the course. This writing experience documents how a student's vision and thinking has broadened throughout the course.

4. "Scrapbooks and Collections" is a multi-media documentation which encourages the student's search and sampling of the environment through teacher-suggested research as well as independent thought. Some collections have included unusual greeting cards, collections of labels and price tags, unusual restaurant menus, accidental or planned Photostats, and placemats.

5. "Copyright Files" include student inventions, documented through illustrations and writings. Students enjoy using an available copyright stamp and develop new drawing tools, painting tools, art surfaces, colors, color applicators, printing devices, building materials and art machines. This area demonstrates the student's ability to look for and design new art ideas; the implication is that all art has not yet been invented or pre-defined, that contributions are still needed from future artists.

The contents of the portfolio demonstrate through writings, diagrams, artworks, and object samples that art requires a combination of thinking and creative activity as middle schoolers search for art in all media. Each portfolio is used throughout the art semester as an evolving storage unit, instead of as a place to simply house completed works and ideas.

The search for art can continue during the middle school years. Classes are not offered as solutions, in knowing how to do art, but as exciting personal adventures in learning to discover art. Students begin to see themselves as artists, inventors, and shoppers searching through a rich variety of art sources.

There is a great rebuilding of student's artistic confidence in knowing that the art world has not been pre-invented for them, that their contributions and ideas are still welcome. At the end of a semester, middle school students are free to voice ideas, tell stories, share finds and observations, and are more open to making things and playing with objects and their environment, playing almost as freely as they used to as children.

RELATED READINGS

Szekely, G. (1993). Visual arts area of study. *Arts resource handbook.* New York: Kraus International Books.

Szekely, G. (1993). Teaching art is about children. *Journal of the Ontario Society for Education Through Art, 22,* 6–17.

Szekely, G. (1993). Adopting-a-school: Art education students in residence. *Art Education, 46(5),* 18–25.

Szekely, G. (1991). *From play to art.* Portsmouth, NH: Heinemann Educational Books.

Szekely, G. (1988). *Encouraging creativity in art lessons.* New York: Teachers College Press.

Students With Special Needs: Creating an Equal Opportunity Classroom

Susan Washam Witten
Ohio Department of Education
The Ohio State University

Students with special needs were given access to public school classrooms in 1975 with the passage of Public Law 94-142. However, twenty years later, some teachers continue to respond to these citizens as outsiders. Middle school teachers are no different. How did the situation come to be and what can be done at the classroom level to provide equal access to art education for all middle school students?

THE SKY IS FALLING

The tale of the fabled fowl whose narrow and short-sighted interpretation of an event was accepted and acted upon has served as a symbol of both myopia and mass hysteria for generations. However, many of us in "regular" education responded the same way when Public Law (PL) 94-142 was enacted. This equal educational opportunity law and its least restrictive environment clause resulted in an influx of children with disabilities into regular schools and classrooms. Some of us hid our heads, some cried doom and gloom, and others responded with prescriptions and panaceas. This initial panic and flurry of activity evolved into reluctant acceptance. Yet twenty years later, we are still concerned with and responding to issues resulting from the interpretation and application of this milestone legislation.

Advocates for the law believed not only that all children have a right to an education but also that if children experiencing disabilities attended regular schools and were given opportunities to be educated and to socialize with "normal" peers, academic improvement and social integration would occur. While the law refers to education "in the least restrictive environment" and does not use the term *main-*

streaming, mainstreaming became synonymous with the integration of children experiencing disabilities into regular education classes.

In practice, the concept of a least restrictive environment is often interpreted as a physical location, rather than a set of conditions that promote normal social interactions and academic growth among students of different abilities. That location, in many cases, has been taken to mean art, music, and physical education classrooms (Atterbury, 1990; Hock, Hasazi, & Patten, 1990). Physical proximity to peers as a primary criteria for placement does not always result in good educational practice. Unfortunately, the goals proponents of PL 94-142 hoped to achieve have often been undermined by such impoverished interpretations (Chandler, 1986; Gresham, 1982; Jellison, Brooks, & Huck, 1984; Madden & Slavin, 1983; White, 1982).

PL 94-142 has had direct implications for teachers of art as a result of mainstreaming and placement practices. For example, a 1992 study (Witten) of Ohio art educators revealed that all middle school art teachers responding to a survey on the status of students with disabilities taught students with identified disabilities and that 78% taught students with specific learning disabilities, 72% taught students with developmental disabilities, 32% taught students with multiple disabilities, and 23% taught students with severe behavioral disabilities. Due to current national trends and legislation, the percentages of students with multiple disabilities and behavioral disabilities are likely to increase.

The Americans with Disabilities Act (1990), civil rights legislation for persons with disabilities, has recently focused attention on some of the "separate but equal" interpretations of the earlier law. Educators at all levels are reexamining the manner in which children with disabilities are provided educational opportunities. One result of this reexamination is the current philosophy of inclusion which espouses that all children of all abilities be included as members of an educational grouping. Instead of being considered as outsiders who are occasionally permitted inside the doors of the privileged, children with disabilities begin their education inside those doors. In theory, students with disabilities are assigned to the classrooms in which they would normally be placed demographically if they did not have disabilities. Classroom teachers and students are then given assistance by special educators both in and outside the classroom (Bilken, Lehr, Searl, & Taylor, 1987; Lipsky & Gartner, 1989; Sayer, 1991).

In addition, the practice of inclusion means that no one classroom or teacher is challenged with instructing artificially high numbers of children with disabilities. The issue of social integration becomes moot when children begin their education naturally as part of the classroom and school population. Unfortunately, like its predecessors "normalization" (Wolfensberger, 1972) and "least restrictive environment," the gap between theory and practice is cavernous. Some school systems are closing down their separate programs one day, and numbers of children with disabilities are attending the "regular" schools the next. Other school districts are renaming their main-

Educators at all levels are re-examining the manner in which children with disabilities are provided educational opportunities.

streaming practices *inclusion* and doing business as usual. Such practices have resulted in an influx of students with severe behavioral, cognitive, and medical disabilities into schools and classrooms which are not adequately equipped and whose staffs have not been prepared for the increased diversity of their students. This misapplication of the concept of inclusion has reignited many of the fears and concerns of the seventies.

Meanwhile art education has evolved beyond the days of minimal instruction and a solitary focus on media experiences. Contemporary art instruction is sequential and includes aesthetics, criticism, and art history along with production; student assessment has shifted from "effort" to "achievement of objectives."

Art teachers in the Ohio study (Witten, 1992) responded to a perceived dichotomy between the needs of students with disabilities and a comprehensive approach to art education. They returned to a more production-based program for classes which included students with disabilities. This diversion from established art education goals was based on the belief that all students can work with art materials, a belief that resulted in the wholesale placement of students with disabilities into art classrooms following passage of PL 94-142. This premise ignores the diversity of students and does all students a disservice by narrowing their art learning possibilities. How then do art teachers shoulder the increasing responsibilities of expanded curriculum content and increased student diversity?

CREATING AN EQUAL OPPORTUNITY CLASSROOM

Balancing education's 20-year history of attempted integration for children with disabilities, the recent refocus on equal rights, the evolution of art education, and the current national focus on educational reform with good practice is challenging. Middle school classrooms often are a microcosm of the larger educational universe and have potential to serve as test environments for instructional strategies to make education work for all children.

Many middle school students are at-risk whether they have an identified disability or not. It is often difficult for learning to occur during the daily battles for peer acceptance, biological control, and self-understanding. The cognitive, developmental, and physical diversity of adolescents in general requires numerous instructional strategies: a classroom management plan, clearly-stated behavioral expectations, communication with other professionals and parents, multiple approaches for instruction and assessment, and, of course, a sense of humor. These strategies are especially important in working with students with disabilities.

> Contemporary art instruction is sequential and includes aesthetics, criticism, and art history along with production; student assessment has shifted from "effort" to "achievement of objectives."

LAYING THE GROUNDWORK

At best, art classrooms are often bustling hives of activity with students moving around to collect or dispose of materials as they work individually and collectively. At worst, art classrooms can be chaotic. In both scenarios, it is easy for some students to become distracted, overstimulated, or confused. Providing a consistent structure for discussion, distribution of materials, movement within the classroom, clean-up, and seating allows all students to keep their focus more clearly on learning. These procedures should be communicated in writing and, periodically, be reinforced orally.

It is equally important to have and consistently enforce clearly stated behavioral expectations and consequences which are compatible with school policy. Although middle school students will often test limits, replacing subjectivity with clear guidelines and consistent enforcement can help reduce such behavior.

Another necessary component of an equal opportunity classroom is frequent communication with other professionals as well as with parents. Consistency is critical at the middle school level; teachers must work together to develop behavioral expectations and consequences and to encourage parents to become partners in the process. Building-level problem-solving groups, such as intervention assistance teams, can help an individual teacher develop instructional and behavioral strategies for problems that go beyond the ordinary. An individual education plan (IEP) is legally mandated for all students with special needs and should be developed with input from all teachers. If art teacher input is not included in the IEP, an information channel must be opened with the special education team. It is as important for the IEP planning team to understand course and classroom expectations in art as it is for the art teacher to be aware of specific adaptations a student may need.

Educators are often concerned about assuming parental roles. However, parents are frequently overlooked as potential educational partners. At the minimum, parents should be informed in writing of policies, expectations, and course requirements; they cannot be expected to support a system unless they are so informed. They can become allies in other ways, as well. Parents can be invaluable sources of information about their own children. Frequently, parents are consulted not when a difficulty surfaces but only after a problem has escalated into a crisis. Inviting parents to share successes and failures, particularly with children with behavioral or multiple disabilities, can be both enlightening and a source of support to the teacher.

INSTRUCTIONAL STRATEGIES

Although laying careful groundwork through teamwork and establishing clear expectations can make the diversity in the middle school art classroom more manageable, the quality of the instructional inter-

> Consistency is critical at the middle school level; teachers must work together to develop behavioral expectations and consequences and to encourage parents to become partners in the process.

action between the teacher and the student is crucial. From theories of multiple intelligences (Gardner, 1983) to those of culture specific learning styles (Stokrocki, 1990), we know that people learn and interact with the world in many different ways. However, educators have attempted to categorize students with disabilities into specific groups and have prescribed certain teaching and learning techniques for each group. Although these techniques may be helpful, it is important to remember that the student with disabilities is a person first, subject to the many influences that can affect learning.

Clearly stated and communicated learning objectives and criteria for assessment are important for all students. Students should know what they are expected to learn and how that learning will be measured. Criteria should be specific and a hierarchy identified.

The process of weighting criteria helps identify what is most important and can be especially helpful in working with students with disabilities. For example, if there are ten criteria to be met to receive an "A," there may be seven for a "B." However, only five may be essential to show an understanding of the most important concepts. While this approach requires the teacher to examine each lesson for those most essential components, it allows the student who works slowly or has difficulty with abstract concepts, opportunities for success.

It is equally important to allow for alternative solutions to the problems or questions posed within the lesson. For example, computer graphics can eliminate the frustration students with physical limitations have experienced in traditional studio activities. Tape and video recorders offer options to students whose ideas are often stifled through difficulty with written expression. All students must have viable options.

An inclusionary approach to the presentation of art content is also required. For some students, the ability to create art is a freeing experience and opens avenues to learning. For others, it may be constricting. Teaching art concepts through critical inquiry, historical inquiry, philosophical inquiry, and studio inquiry offers students of all abilities and learning styles opportunities to learn about art.

Specific instructional approaches used by special education teachers in their classrooms are applicable to the art classroom and can help make art more accessible to identified and unidentified students with special needs:

1. Printed materials, including teacher made hand-outs should be printed on white paper with bold black ink. Colored paper and gray or colored print are distracting and, for some students, impossible to read. Highlighting or underlining important points assists students who are overwhelmed by masses of print or have difficulty discerning critical concepts. An outline, enlarged type, or an audio recording may be needed for students with visual disabilities or perception problems. Providing lectures or instructions in outline form on paper or on tape can also benefit

Students should know what they are expected to learn and how that learning will be measured.

students who wish to revisit a point or who may have been absent.

2. Make use of technology when presenting material to the class. Reinforce lectures, instructions, and discussions with hand-outs and overheads. When using slides or reproductions, have copies that can be examined at close range for students with visual disabilities or perception problems. Art reproductions on computer disc also allow a close look at images. Some students may find black and white reproductions helpful in discerning specific elements. Reproductions with raised lines or other textures can provide a general idea of an image for students who are severely visually impaired. Become familiar with audio assistance technology and other assistive devices available to students with hearing impairments or communication difficulties by contacting the speech therapist, audiologist, or special education teacher.

3. During class discussions, enforce rules of conduct so that only one person speaks at a time. Restate important ideas and concepts and have an appointed recorder transcribe them on an overhead projector. It may be helpful to record discussions for some students. In the process of aesthetic, art criticism, and art history activities, students frequently begin exploring concrete concepts and move toward the more interpretive and abstract. Allow students with cognitive disabilities opportunities to participate at the early levels of discussion. Once engaged, they are more likely to follow the direction of the class.

4. When demonstrating a studio skill, make sure students have a clear line of vision. Small group demonstrations are generally more effective because students can examine the materials and are less distracted. Demonstrations should be explained step-by-step in clear, concise terminology. Special vocabulary should be included on a hand-out which provides step-by-step instructions; this type of hand-out can be very helpful in working with students who need concepts broken down or to be frequently redirected to the task. Directions should also be available on tape for those students unable to read print. Students who are visually impaired may need one-on-one instruction; however, inviting them to participate in the demonstration through tactile examination of each step can give them access to the instruction and offer the other students new insights into the process. For students who have coordination and strength problems, explore the options of helmets and headpieces, mouth-held tools, braces, and other adaptive tools with the appropriate resource teachers and therapists.

5. Offer a range of materials during the studio process to better meet student ability levels. In addition to two- and three-dimensional computer design techniques, numerous other possibilities exist. Paper can be taped to tables, tools can be padded and wrapped, texture can be added to paint, and foams can replace

In the process of aesthetic, art criticism, and art history activities, students frequently begin exploring concrete concepts and move toward the more interpretive and abstract.

less pliable materials. However, do not rule out the student's interest in trying to work with any materials. Allow opportunities; problem-solve together. Consider the conceptual art process where the artist describes the idea and directs someone else's hands.

6. There are always materials to be distributed and collected, reproductions and artwork to be shown, and discussions to be recorded on the board or overhead projector. Use these opportunities to provide the student "who cannot sit still" an option to move around in an acceptable way. For students with a history of violent or destructive behavior, become familiar with their crisis intervention plans and be prepared to implement them.

7. Seek consultation from the IEP team, school nurse, or family if there is a student with serious health problems. For example, the dust and fumes from certain art products could have adverse effects on a student with an assistive breathing device.

8. Evaluate the physical environment in terms of adverse conditions which could affect the learning of all students. Can students move around without jostling each other? Does a student who uses mobility assistance have room to navigate? Are the tables appropriate heights for children with physical disabilities? Are students with visual disabilities and perception problems facing away from the glare of a window? Are students with hearing impairments seated near the front of the room where they are less distracted by classroom noise and have a clear view of the teacher? Are students with attention deficits or with behavioral disabilities seated close to the teacher and away from obvious distractions such as the hallway, windows, materials, and supplies? Are students with disabilities seated among the other students so that all can benefit from peer interaction? Consult the resource teacher, school administrator, or intervention assistance team if you need help in solving these or other potential problems.

CONCLUSION

Students with disabilities are citizens and people first. Being an integral member of the learning community is their right and of particular importance during adolescence when acceptance by peers is important. By treating each student as an individual and unique learner, clarifying expectations and critical concepts, varying instructional approaches, organizing the classroom, communicating with others, and adapting materials, the middle school art teacher can enhance learning opportunities for all students. In doing so, an equal opportunity classroom can become a reality.

Students with disabilities are citizens and people first.

REFERENCES

Americans with Disabilities Act. of 1990, 42 USC §12101.

Atterbury, B. W. (1990). *Mainstreaming exceptional learners in music*. Englewood Cliff, NJ: Prentice-Hall.

Bilken, D., Lehr, S., Searl, S. J., & Taylor, S. J. (1987). *Purposeful integration . . . inherently equal.* Boston: Technical Assistance for Parents Programs.

Chandler, H. N. (1986). Mainstreaming: A formative consideration. *Journal of Learning Disabilities, 19*(2), 125–126.

Gardner, H. (1983). *Frames of mind.* New York: Basic Books.

Gresham, F. M. (1982). Misguided mainstreaming: The case for special skill training with handicapped children. *Exceptional Children, 48*(5), 422–433.

Hock, M., Hasazi, R. B., & Patton, A. (1990). Collaboration through learning: Strategies for program success. *Music Educators Journal, 76*(8), 44–48.

Jellison, J. A., Brooks, B. H., & Huck, A. M. (1984). Structuring small groups and music reinforcement to facilitate positive interactions and acceptance of severely handicapped students in the regular music classroom. *Journal of Research in Music Education, 32*(4), 243–264.

Lipsky, D. K., & Gartner, A. (Eds.). (1989). *Beyond separate education.* Baltimore: Paul H. Brooks.

Madden, N. A., & Slavin, R. E. (1983). Mainstreaming students with mild handicaps: Academic and social outcomes. *Review of Educational Research, 53*, 519–573.

Public Law 94–142. (1975). *Federal Register*, Tuesday, August 23, 1975.

Sayer, J. (1991). A whole school approach to meeting all needs. In G. Grant (Ed.), *Review of Research in Education, Vol.17.* Washington, D.C.: American Educational Research Association.

Stokrocki, M. (1990). Issues in multicultural art education. In E. W. King & S. D. La Pierre (Eds.), *Using the arts as an educational model for high risk individuals* (pp. 34–41). Denver, CO: University of Denver Press.

White, L. D. (1982). How to adapt for special needs learners. *Music Educators Journal, 68*(8), 49–50, 63.

Witten, S. W. (1992). A study and analysis of art education in Ohio for K–8 children experiencing disabilities. (Doctoral dissertation, The Ohio State University, 1991). *Dissertation Abstracts International, 52*(11), 3808.

Wolfensberger, W. (1972). *The principle of normalization in human services.* Toronto: National Institute on Mental Retardation.

Building a Foundation for Assessment: Eight Questions To Guide Our Planning

INTRODUCTION

Eldon Katter with Marilyn Stewart
Kutztown University

With each new wave of assessment literature comes rising expectations about what assessment can accomplish. Riding the crest of one wave are those who see the primary purpose of major assessment efforts as gathering data on how well schools are doing. People want to know how one school district compares to another, how one state compares to another, and how we as a nation compare to other nations (Loyacono, 1992). Within this group of educators are those who make reference to collecting information through standardized testing and those who consider assessment in terms of evaluating teaching behaviors, the strengths and weaknesses of the curriculum, and instruction.

In the wake of another wave, the results of assessment are being tied to student promotion and graduation requirements. Among this group are educators who write about assessment in terms of collecting information about what students know and understand about art and who imply that collecting information about what students know about art is synonymous with collecting student art work.

Obviously, there are multiple purposes and multiple means for assessment which more often than not lead to confused purposes and unproductive ways of working. There are many right reasons, and there are multiple ways, for assessing. But not all types of assessment are appropriate for all purposes. For example, portfolios are especially applicable to the assessment of individual and class or group progress in art and not as useful at the state level for determining how well schools are doing. Given present conditions, portfolios are most appropriately analyzed at the classroom and school levels.

However, when statewide outcomes are in place, when all districts have clearly identified culminating demonstrations of success, and when all teachers have had adequate professional development train-

In building a foundation for assessment, we should make sure our footing is based solidly on the belief that all students can succeed and that schools create the conditions for success (Spady & Marshall, 1991).

ing in portfolio assessment, then it might be possible to use portfolios in statewide assessment. We need to first build a good foundation. That takes time.

How do we prevent assessment programs from becoming burdensome and confusing? The answer is, quite simply, to make assessment an integral and carefully aligned component of the instructional plan from the very beginning. As with any good teaching strategy, we must make sure we adequately cover the material, provide ample practice for mastery, test, re-teach, and re-test for success before moving on to the next level. We first build a foundation for assessment planning that focuses on student demonstrations of success and includes assessment tasks that approximate meaningful, real-life learning experiences.

In building a foundation for assessment, we should make sure our footing is based solidly on the belief that all students can succeed and that schools create the conditions for success (Spady & Marshall, 1991). As we build upward, we define the substance of the discipline, including inquiry processes and settings. We identify culminating demonstrations of success and include the assessment criteria, rubrics, and levels of achievement.

GUIDELINES FOR ASSESSMENT PLANNING

The following eight questions can serve as our guidelines for building a foundation for assessment planning in art:

1. *What settings are appropriate for student learning?* To ensure that learning takes place in appropriate, significant, and authentic settings, we must pay attention to psychological, physical, and social contexts. We then should consider various group configurations from individual projects to large-group audiences. What we may find is that appropriate settings extend beyond classroom walls and into the community.
2. *What major concepts and principles are essential to student understanding of art?* To ensure that the art program has significant substance, we need to identify broad, interrelated concepts and principles among content areas such as art studio, art criticism, art history, and aesthetics. We then can focus on the products, ideas, and concerns of people whose lives are devoted to art. What we may find is that our major concepts—the substance of what is to be taught—can be simply stated as follows:
   a. Art has meaning.
   b. Art is created and responded to in context.
   c. Art is thoughtfully created through expression and reflection.
   d. Art reflects and is influenced by philosophical beliefs.
3. *What skills are most appropriate for engaging students in the demonstration of this knowledge in art?* To ensure that the scope of art learning encompasses significant skills, we must

examine the inquiry processes used by artists, critics, historians, and philosophers. We can then focus on the appropriate procedural knowledge—the ways of knowing, the ways of constructing meaning, and the ways of constructing models for inquiry that are discipline specific (Marzano, 1992). What we may find is that the methods of inquiry to be developed and practiced through the study of art can be stated as follows:

a. Artists, critics, historians, and philosophers are skilled at constructing, interpreting, and organizing meaning; storing and recalling information; constructing models for procedures; and shaping and internalizing procedures.

b. People who are successful in art extend and refine operations through questioning, comparing, classifying, induction, deduction, reflection, constructing support, analyzing perspectives, and abstracting.

c. People involved in the arts apply the skills of decision making, investigation, experimental inquiry, problem-solving, and invention.

d. Successful artists, critics, historians, and aestheticians engage in productive work habits involving a balance in self-regulatory, creative, and critical thinking.

4. *Based on the assumptions we have made about settings, substance, and skills, what are the outcomes of an education in art?* By combining the substance and skills identified earlier, we can begin to focus on outcome statements. The outcomes identify what students can do successfully by the time they exit their schooling:

a. Art has meaning. Meaning is accessible to students, like critics, through learned procedures such as description, analysis, interpretation, and judgment. With proper instruction, all students can learn to arrive at plausible meanings, interpretations, and evaluations of works of art.

b. Art is created and responded to in context. Contextual relationships can be described by students, like art historians, through investigation of social, historical, and psychological factors. Well-designed instruction can enable all students to engage in inquiry into the relationships between art, history, and culture.

c. Art is thoughtfully created through expression and reflection. Students, like artists, can create thoughtfully, expressively, and reflectively as they develop productive habits of mind. Through carefully sequenced studio exercises, all students can learn to approach the creation of artworks by reflecting on personal beliefs, considering cultural values and human needs, constructing meanings, expressing ideas, and developing technical skills.

d. Art reflects and is influenced by philosophical beliefs.

> Successful artists, critics, historians, and aestheticians engage in productive work habits involving a balance in self-regulatory, creative, and critical thinking.

Philosophical beliefs can be examined as students, like philosophers, question and analyze perspectives. In non-threatening and supportive instructional settings, all students can be taught to reflect upon beliefs about art and to inquire about the relationship between art and human experience.

As we continue to refine and articulate an outcome, we might want to apply the following checklist questions: Is the outcome based on disciplined inquiry? Is it a reflection of the knowledge, competencies, and orientations needed by adults in a diverse, complex, and changing society? Is it a culminating demonstration of learning that really matters? Is the outcome clearly defined, so that everyone has a clear picture of the target and can recognize success when they see it? Is it success oriented, allowing for more than one chance for students to be successful? Is it approachable from a rich diversity of instructional methods and assessment strategies? Have students and other members of the educational community been involved in the process of identifying outcomes?

5. *How do we prepare students for success?* In building an assessment foundation, outcomes, instruction, and assessment are carefully aligned. Instruction is the process for providing learning experiences necessary for achievement of the stated learner outcomes. The instructional process utilizes a variety of teaching models, methods, and materials. Instruction can involve lecture, reading, audio-visual media, demonstration, discussion groups, practice, and teaching others. The process provides for prerequisites, cue-setting, guided practice, independent practice, correctives, diversions, re-focusing, re-teaching, reviews, enrichments and extensions, and closure. As we identify intended outcomes, we simultaneously develop our instructional plans. In developing instructional plans, the following questions can serve as a checklist for appropriateness: Does the instructional activity attend to both processes and products of teaching and learning? Does it inform students of the criteria for evaluation? Does it provide models of the standards of achievement? Does the activity incorporate assessment as part of the learning process? Is self-assessment a part of the instructional plan? Will the student be able to find value in the activity in and of itself and apart from whether it is being assessed? Are there alternative ways to approach the tasks?

6. *What kinds of authentic assessment tasks can be designed?* Diversified assessment entails the use of multiple assessment strategies to gather information about the progress of students. For each of the outcomes in our course of study in art, we could then design authentic assessments. This would give students opportunities to demonstrate knowledge of content and progress toward larger, broader learner outcomes. These assessment assignments would eventually provide the tangible evi-

The instructional process utilizes a variety of teaching models, methods, and materials.

dence students will use for performance-based graduation requirements. We must design our assessment tasks as we develop our instructional plans. We can then apply the following checklist: Does the assessment strategy evaluate students on tasks that approximate discipline inquiry? Are we employing standards based on widely accepted norms in the discipline? Have we considered knowledge and skills holistically rather than in fragmented parts? Are we measuring more than factual recall? Does the task simulate an actual performance of a complex skill in context close to how it would be used in real life? Is there a self-assessment component? Does the task allow for multiple approaches to success?

Following are examples of broad categories of assessment strategies that might be used collectively to produce a performance profile of student success: observation, interview, individual inventory, performance, pencil and paper tests, essay, journal or diary, and folio.

7. *What criteria will we use for measuring success?* For each of our outcomes, we should establish a set of three or four criteria to guide performance. These descriptions of competent performance characteristics are based on the substance and the skills which drive the outcome. For example, performance characteristics for competently arriving at meaning in works of art might be (a) compares and classifies subject matter and other elements in the work, (b) constructs meaning from an account of the work, and (c) constructs support for an evaluation of the work. These characteristics remain the same for all grade levels. While a tenth grader might compare and classify subject matter with descriptive, qualitative language, a fifth grader might use a simpler vocabulary, and a first grader might physically group works of like subject matter without naming.

8. *What rubric will we use for rating the student performance?* For each of these criteria, we can establish means of scoring such as this four-step scoring guide (called NICE):
Novice performer—level 1.
Improved performer—level 2.
Competent performer—level 3 (TARGET) all must reach.
Exceptional performer—level 4 exemplary.

Stated in positive, success-oriented language, these descriptors for rating student achievement are consistent throughout all grade levels. An eighth grader who consistently compares and classifies subject matter with simple, but accurate, vocabulary might be considered a competent performer on one characteristic. A novice performer at the eighth grade level might sometimes classify similar subjects but not always describe the categories with accuracy. Improved performance might be demonstrated through vocabulary development.

For each of the outcomes in our course of study in art, we could then design authentic assessments.

A solid assess—
ment foundation
has a framework
of criteria and
descriptive
rubrics, all
developed from
stated outcomes.

CONCLUSION

A solid assessment foundation has a framework of criteria and descriptive rubrics, all developed from stated outcomes. It focuses on student success and provides an instructional plan for both educators and students. It provides teachers with flexibility of choice within the framework while requiring consistency of standards. Students know what is expected.

The result is improved instruction and improved learning. Students are engaged in their own learning because the tasks they are given are meaningful and intriguing. Knowing the assessment criteria up front, students take responsibility for becoming prepared and using resources. More active student involvement in interesting tasks results in improved learning.

NOTE

Eldon Katter and Marilyn Stewart are Professors of Art Education at Kutztown University, Kutztown, Pennsylvania. This chapter is developed from the outline of a teacher in-service workshop which Katter and Stewart have presented jointly on several occasions.

REFERENCES

Loyacono, L. (1992). *Reinventing the wheel: A design for student achievement in the 21st century.* Washington, DC: National Conference of State Legislatures.

Marzano, R. (1992). *A different kind of classroom: Teaching with dimensions of learning.* Alexandria, VA: Association for Supervision and Curriculum Development.

Spady, W. and Marshall, K. (1991). Beyond traditional outcome-based education. *Educational Leadership, 49* (2), 67-72.